Discover & Learn

Science

Years One & Two

This Teacher Book is for use alongside CGP's Science **Study and Activity Books**. It has everything you'll need to teach the Science Programme of Study for Key Stage One.

In the **Teacher Book**, you'll find detailed lesson plans, including ideas for extension, assessment and follow-up activities.

The **CD-ROM** includes a huge range of printable resources, plus full IWB versions of the Activity Books.

We have included useful web links in this Teacher Book — we can't take responsibility for the content of these external sites, so please check that the content is suitable before you use them with the children. Please also ensure they are supervised when researching material online.

Introduction

Range Overview

Discover & Learn is a flexible and easy-to-use resource to help you teach KS1 Science.

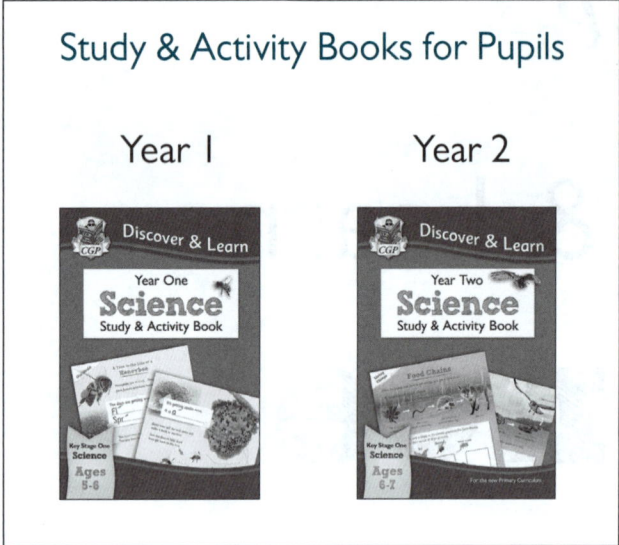

Study & Activity Books

The Study & Activity Books introduce and explain the scientific concepts to pupils and check their understanding.

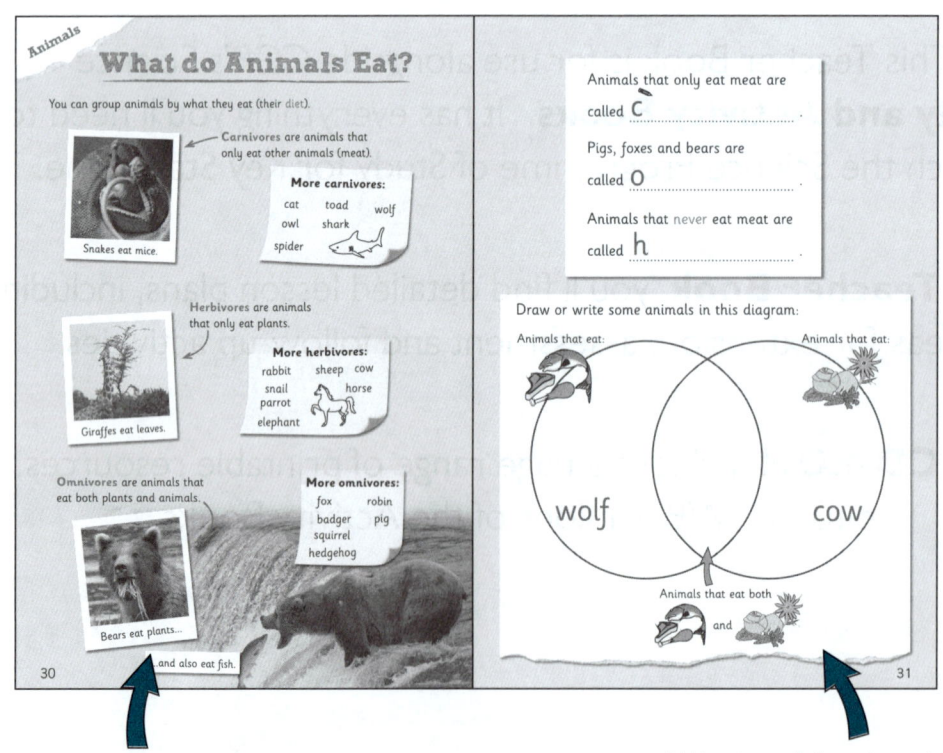

Illustrations and explanations of the key concepts from the KS1 Science Programme of Study.

Write-in and draw-in activities for pupils to demonstrate their understanding.

Introduction

Teacher Book

The Teacher Book provides detailed lesson plans for each topic of the Activity Book.

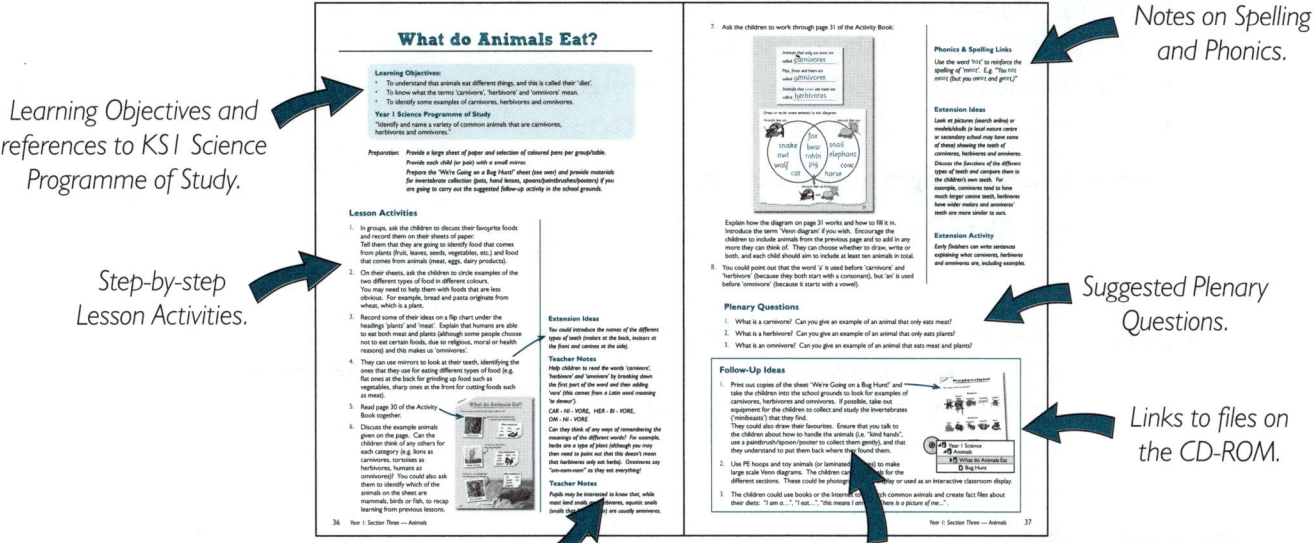

Learning Objectives and references to KS1 Science Programme of Study.

Step-by-step Lesson Activities.

Ideas for extension and extra teacher guidance.

Notes on Spelling and Phonics.

Suggested Plenary Questions.

Links to files on the CD-ROM.

Follow-Up Ideas for subsequent lessons.

The Teacher Book also provides detailed Assessment Notes at the end of each section.

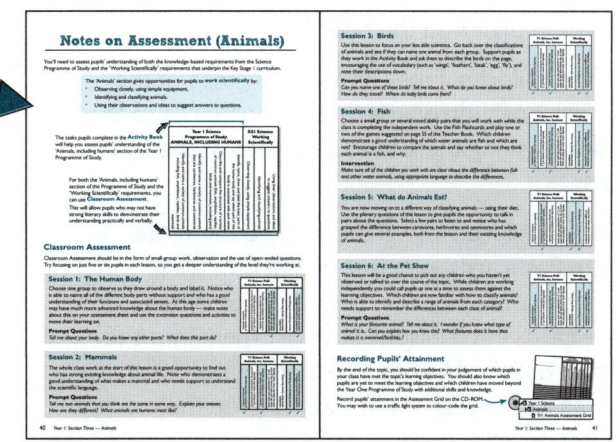

CD-ROM

The CD-ROM contains lots of additional resources.

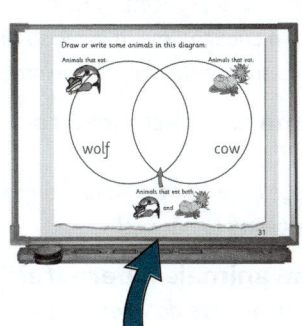

PowerPoint® slides of every page of the Activity Books enable you to display the pages on an interactive whiteboard.

(You can annotate the slides, and 'Save As' if you want to keep these annotations.)

Slideshows and printable worksheets and flashcards supplement the Lesson and Follow-Up Activities.

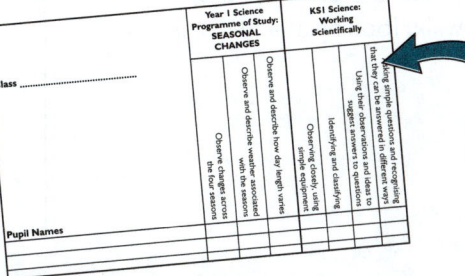

The CD-ROM also has printable and editable Assessment Grids so you can chart pupils' progress through each topic.

Introduction 3

Year 1: Section One — Our World
Changing Seasons

Learning Objectives:
- To learn the names of the four seasons.
- To describe what happens in each of the different seasons.
- To sort the months of the year into the correct seasons.

Year 1 Science Programme of Study

"Observe changes across the four seasons."

Preparation: Take the children on a walk and ask them to pay particular attention to the trees and flowers. Take photographs along the way in order to describe them later. Prepare the flash cards (on CD-ROM).

Lesson Activities

1. Ask the children to name the months of the year. Using the flashcards on the CD-ROM, put the months in order on the board.

2. Ask the children if they know the names of the four seasons. Introduce the season words to the children, asking them to repeat each of the words.

3. Split the children into groups. Give them the month flashcards, pictures of different trees and other seasonal pictures. Ask them to group these cards into seasons and sort them into the correct order. They should then explain their choices to the rest of the class. Agree the correct order as a class.

4. Ask the children which month of the year their birthday is in. Ask them to talk to the person next to them about which season this is in.

5. Ask them to discuss if there are any other celebrations during the season in which their birthday falls, e.g. Christmas, Diwali, Easter. Encourage children to share their experiences of their own religious festivals.

6. Read the information from the top half of pages 2 and 3 of the Activity Book together.

7. Discuss which season we are in now and how we know this. Refer to the information given in the Activity Book, as well as the evidence they gathered on their walk, looking at and discussing the photos taken.

Extension Activity
The pupils could write a sentence about each of the seasons. E.g. "In summer we can visit the beach."

Phonics & Spelling Links
Use the words 'winter', 'summer' and 'hibernate' when teaching the 'schwa' sound (/ə/). Also, encourage pupils to notice the silent letters in 'lamb' and 'autumn'.

Extension Questions

"Why do you think many baby animals are born in spring?"
They are born as the weather is getting warmer. This should give them enough time to grow, so they are strong enough to survive the following winter.

"Why is autumn the best time to harvest crops?"
By the autumn, crops have had the whole summer to grow, so there is plenty to harvest!

"Why do some animals hibernate?"
Explain to pupils that animals do whatever they can to survive. Winter is a difficult time for many animals, because it is cold and there isn't much food. Some animals save their energy by hibernating. They allow their heartbeats to slow down, and their body temperatures to drop.

8. Ask the pupils to complete the activities in the Activity Book:

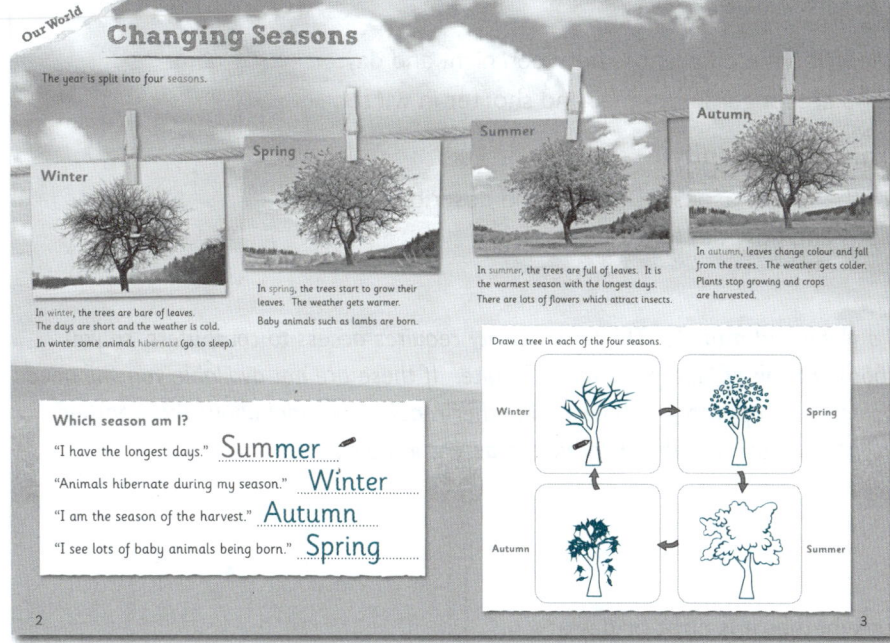

Extension Questions

"Which animals hibernate? Where do they hibernate?"

Bats hibernate in large trees, caves, old wells, and even in people's attics. Depending on the species of bat, they either hibernate alone or in groups. Hedgehogs hibernate from a few weeks to a few months depending on the weather. They build themselves nests under hedges, in trees roots or in compost heaps. Dormice hibernate too — they roll themselves into a ball in a nest of grass and leaves.

Extension Activity

Pupils could write their own clues for "Which season am I?" e.g. "I am when the leaves fall from the trees."

Pupils could now use the information from the Activity Book to draw a picture to represent one of the seasons.

Plenary Questions

1. What are the names of the four seasons?
2. Which months fall in which season?
3. What happens to the trees in the different seasons?
4. What can you say about animals during the different seasons?

Follow-Up Ideas

1. Children could keep a diary of activity in their garden or in the playground to show changes over time. Less able pupils could keep a photo diary.

2. As a class, make a tally chart of the number of children who have a birthday in each season and convert their data into a bar chart.

3. Children could learn about the different festivals which fall in different seasons e.g. Diwali, Easter, Christmas. As a class, research a festival on the Internet. The pupils could then make a greetings card for their favourite festival.

4. Read 'One Year With Kipper' by Mick Inkpen. Pupils could draw pictures of something they might photograph during each month of the year.

Night and Day

> **Learning Objectives:**
> - To understand and describe the differences between night and day.
> - To investigate why days are longer in summer and shorter in winter.
>
> **Year 1 Science Programme of Study**
> "Observe changes across the four seasons. Observe and describe weather associated with the seasons and how day length varies."

Preparation: You will need a globe and a torch. The final activity requires access to computers, so you may need to book a bank of laptops or the ICT suite. If these are not available you will need to provide a selection of appropriate books and other reading material about the weather, seasons and night and day, that the children can access in pairs.

Lesson Activities

1. Ask the children to think about whether it is night or day at the moment. How can they tell? What information do we need to know if it is night or day? Note any suggestions on the white board.

2. Clear a space in the classroom or alternatively go to a hall or outside. Print off two signs saying "night" and "day" from the CD-ROM and stick them on opposite sides of the room. Read out statements that relate to either night or day. Children have to run to the correct side of the room, depending on the clue.
Statements could include:
It is dark. It is sunny. I can see stars. We are at school. The flowers are open. We have all the lights on.
You could also include some more ambiguous ones such as:
It is raining. People are at work.
Discuss these and any questions that they raise.

3. Now make your classroom as dark as possible and ask the class to sit in a circle. Ask one pupil to stand in the centre with a torch or lamp representing the Sun. Stand a metre away from the 'Sun' holding a small globe and use some coloured tape to mark the UK.

4. Spin the globe and demonstrate that when the UK is facing towards the Sun it is light and daytime, when it is facing away it is dark and night.

5. Now slowly begin to orbit the Sun, whilst continuing to spin the globe on its axis. (Make sure you keep the North Pole pointing in the same direction.) You are demonstrating that when our part of the Earth is tilted away from the Sun, it is winter and the days are short, when we are tilted towards the Sun it is summer and the days are longer. This is a confusing concept, so you might want to repeat it a few times and have different pupils have a go at being the Sun and the Earth.

Key Facts

- The Earth spins on its axis.
- One full spin takes 24 hours, or one full day and night.
- The Earth is tilted (by 23.5 degrees), but the North Pole always points in the same direction.
- The Earth orbits the Sun. (The Sun does not move around the Earth.)
- One full orbit takes 365 days, or a year.

Extension Ideas

Show the animation 'Explore a model of Earth's yearly revolution around the Sun', within 'Chapter 4' on this web page:
www.classzone.com/books/earth_science/terc/navigation/visualization.cfm
Click 'Show Labels' to see the months of the year.

6. Read page 4 of the Activity Book together and deal with any misconceptions. Ask pupils to complete page 5 of the Activity Book.

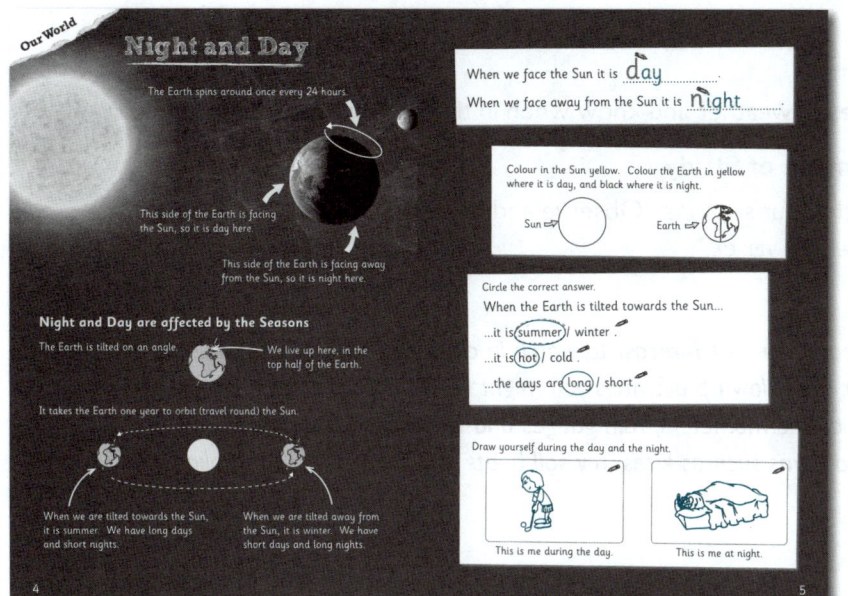

7. Demonstrate some of the different features of the website www.timeanddate.com — a fantastic resource for investigating night and day. The pupils could then:
   - explore the live world maps and find out where it is currently day and night;
   - investigate what the weather is like in different countries and what time it is in other places in the world;
   - look up your location to get information about sunrise and sunset, how it is changing over the week, and the Moon's position.

   At the end of the session, some pupils may want to share their findings with the class, or you could ask each pair to discuss and share something they have learned during the lesson.

Teacher Notes

For this activity you will need access to a bank of computers. Note that it is not expected that all pupils will be able to correctly use and understand the different parts of this site. The important thing is that they are allowed time to try and engage with some of the features of the site and discover something for themselves. It is up to you how much guidance you give during the activity.

You may wish to coincide this lesson with a maths topic on telling the time and some additional learning about countries of the world.

Extension Ideas

You could ask pupils to think of questions that they would like to ask about this topic and stick them on a 'Wonder Wall', to be researched later.

Plenary Questions

1. How can we tell if it is night or day?
2. During what season are the days longest / shortest?
3. Explain to your partner why days are longer in the summer.

Follow-Up Ideas

1. Continue to look at and investigate the globe and the position of different countries and relate it to their time zones. This would be a great way to involve any children who have families from different parts of the world.

2. Use the 'Sunrise and Sunset' worksheet on the CD-ROM to record the changing day length. You can find sunrise and sunset times using the website from the final lesson activity.

3. Learn about the solstices. What do they mean and why are they celebrated? Look at photos of Stonehenge during the summer and winter solstices.

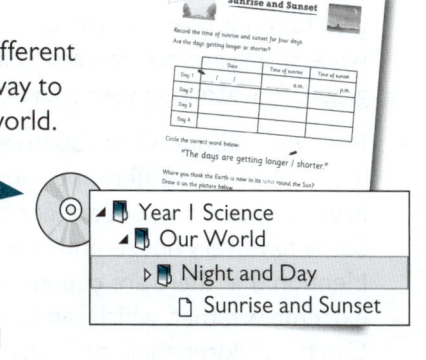

Year 1: Section One — Our World 7

What's the Weather?

> **Learning Objectives:**
> - To name different types of weather and know when in the year they are likely to occur.
>
> **Year 1 Science Programme of Study**
> "Observe changes across the four seasons. Observe and describe weather associated with the seasons and how day length varies."

Preparation: *Find a recent weather report/forecast to watch in class. There are lots available on BBC iPlayer. For the follow up activities you might like to collect a selection of equipment such as thermometers, rain gauges and weather vanes, as well as some weather-powered items such as kites, toy sail boats and solar powered appliances.*

Lesson Activities

1. Ask the children to name as many different types of weather as they can. Discuss these as a class — what is it like to be outside in all the different types? Would you expect to see them at a particular time of year, or do they occur all year-round? Link this back to the seasons, and the weather associated with each one. This website could be helpful: www.weatherwizkids.com

2. Read page 6 of the Activity Book together.

3. Reinforce the fact that the weather is variable (especially in the UK, as we are an island), but that generally it is colder in winter and hotter in summer, while spring and autumn are 'changing' seasons. It gets gradually warmer in spring and cooler in autumn.

4. Briefly talk about other countries where they have weather which is different to ours. Some countries have rainy seasons, but are dry for the rest of the year. Some have very hot summers and very cold winters. Mention that there are countries that experience extreme weather, which can be very dangerous. Can the children think of any examples? (Hurricanes, droughts, extreme temperatures, etc.)

Extension Questions

- People often go on holiday during the summer. Why do you think that is?
- Why do Christmas cards often have snowmen on them?
- What do you think is meant by 'April Showers'?

Extension Ideas

A maths lesson would be a great time to focus on taking the temperature. You could use thermometers to take the temperature outside each day for a week and then plot a graph. This is also a good way to introduce negative numbers on a number line. Explain that when the temperature gets to 0 degrees it is freezing. There is an interactive thermometer here:
www.mathsisfun.com/measure/thermometer.html

5. Ask the pupils to complete page 7 of the Activity Book.

6. Show the class a clip of a recent weather report/forecast. Discuss what information is given in the report and the sort of language that is used. Note any key phrases on the board, for children to refer to later.

7. Split the children into groups or pairs and allocate them each a season. Ask the groups to talk about what the weather might be like on a typical day in that season.

8. Pupils can then work together to prepare a short weather report for a day in that season, using the key phrases for support and the information in the Activity Book as reminders of the different types of weather.

9. Ask the pupils to present their weather report to the class. Can the other children guess what season their report is from? Why? What were the clues?

Teacher Notes

Less able groups should focus on the weather words: is it raining / windy / sunny? Hot or cold? They might include information about what you could do on a day like today. Would you go to the beach or stay indoors? What clothes might you need to wear?

Extension Ideas

Encourage more able groups to give specific information, such as the temperature and wind speed / direction. They might like to use relevant books or websites to research this information.

Plenary Questions

1. What are the different types of weather we can have? Can you name 6?
2. What months are likely to be hottest or coldest?
3. What do you think the weather might be like on your birthday? Why?

Follow-Up Ideas

1. Do some real weather observation. Use a rain gauge, a weather vane and a thermometer to take recordings of the weather in your local environment.

2. Research weather around the world.
   Which countries have very distinct seasons and where in the world is it hot or cold all year round?
   Where in the world would you go for a white Christmas?
   Where would you go for a hot summer holiday?
   Where does it rain the most?
   Where does it rain the least?

3. Pupils could keep weather diaries for a week and note the weather each day. Was it the same all week or did it change? Was the weather what you would expect for this time of year or different? What was their favourite and least favourite weather and why?

4. Look at how the weather can be used to harness energy. This can be done on a small scale in the classroom by making pinwheels and kites and by looking at solar powered lights. You could also look at pictures of wind farms, water wheels and solar panels and talk about alternative energy sources and why these are good for the planet.

A Year in the Life of a Honeybee

> 'A Year in the Life of a Honeybee' is a **synoptic topic** for the Our World section. It builds on the concepts introduced in the preceding sessions and applies them to a real-world context. This lesson could be the starting point for a cross-curricular project on bees.
>
> **Learning Objectives:**
> - To understand how plants and animals change with the seasons.
> - To know some of the changes that happen to honeybees during each season.
>
> **Year 1 Science Programme of Study**
> "Observe changes across the four seasons. Observe and describe weather associated with the seasons and how day length varies."

Preparation: Find a picture of a honeybee to show the children, either in a book or on the Internet. You may need to book a school hall or larger space for the dance section of the lesson.

Lesson Activities

1. Show the class a picture of a honeybee. Ask the pupils what it is and to discuss in pairs what they already know about bees (e.g. what colours they are, that they sting, that they make honey). Share ideas. Can they think of any questions to ask about bees? (Children might ask questions such as how they make honey, where they live, how they fly etc.) Note down their questions so you can refer back to them during the plenary.

2. Show this clip about honeybees:
   www.youtube.com/watch?v=B2jfMHWYTDk
   Alternatively you could use this clip:
   www.youtube.com/watch?v=bArNmKbYVm8

3. Explain that you are going to be looking at a year in the life of a honeybee and what happens to bees during each season. Read pages 8-9 of the Activity Book together, and ask pupils to complete the writing and drawing activities.

Extension Activity

The clips might help to answer some of the questions that pupils asked at the start of the lesson. You could ask more-able pupils to watch out for this information and note it down on a mini-whiteboard as they watch.

Extension Activity

Have a look at the website: www.ngkids.co.uk/animals/Honey-Bees

Children who finish early can try and answer the questions they came up with at the start of the lesson using the information given on this site.

4. Clear space in your classroom or go to the school hall. You are going to make up a class 'Honeybee Dance' that shows what bees do during each season.

10   Year 1: Section One — Our World

5. It is up to you how much you direct the class dance and how much you get children to choreograph sections themselves. You could let pupils work in pairs to come up with different moves and motifs to represent the bees in each season and then bring the best of these together. The important thing is that the dance has four clear sections and that pupils gain a strong understanding of how bee behaviour changes through the seasons and why.

Here are some dance ideas:

Winter: Select a child to be 'the queen'. The rest of the class gathers around the queen to keep warm. Pupils curl up on the floor and shiver gently.

Spring: Some children could be flowers slowly opening, while other children are bees beginning to buzz around the room, visiting the flowers to collect nectar. The queen starts to lay eggs.

Summer: Bees do a waggle dance to show their fellow workers where the best sources of nectar are.
You can see what a waggle dance looks like here:
video.nationalgeographic.com/video/weirdest-bees-dance

Autumn: The bees, having collected food and water for the hive, slow down and begin to die. The queen slows down laying eggs and any remaining bees fly back to the hive, ready for winter.

Music Playlist
Here some pieces of music with which you may like to accompany your 'Honeybee Dance':
Winter: 'Snow, Moon, and Flowers' from *Night Pieces* by Peter Sculthorpe
Spring: 'Morning Mood' from *Peer Gynt Suite No. 1* by Edvard Grieg
Summer: 'Bumble Boogie' by B Bumble and The Stingers
Autumn: 'Sanctus' from *Requiem* by Gabriel Fauré

Performance
After some practice, it would be lovely to perform your class honeybee dance to either another class or to parents. You could select some children to be narrators, explaining what is happening during each season.

Plenary Questions

1. Why do you think bees stay in their hives during winter?

2. Why do we say someone is as busy as a bee?
   During which season are bees at their busiest? Why?

3. How many of the questions that we asked at the start of the lesson have we managed to answer?
   What else would you like to find out?

Follow-Up Ideas

1. Visit an area with lots of wild flowers and do some bee spotting (beware of allergies and ensure safety precautions are taken when observing bees). You could also contact your local beekeeping association to invite a local beekeeper to come in and talk to the class.

2. If your classroom has a patio area you could plant a small bee garden in pots, including plants such as lavender, Sweet William, thyme and chives.

3. Investigate why some bees are dying. What is the impact of honeybees dying on our planet?
   This website is a good starting point:
   www.funkidslive.com/features/a-to-z-of-food-health-and-the-environment/b-for-plan-bee/
   And here is another good article for children: htekidsnews.com/the-secret-death-of-bees/

4. Read the Winnie the Pooh story 'In which we are introduced', which has Pooh trying to track down some honey by pretending to be a little black rain cloud. You could also talk about why bees sting and what we can do to stop ourselves from being stung during the summer.

5. Have a honey picnic — you could either cook with honey or make honey cakes to eat outside.
   It would be great to do this alongside the performance of your 'Honeybee Dance'!

Notes on Assessment (Our World)

You'll need to assess pupils' understanding of both the knowledge-based requirements from the Science Programme of Study and the 'Working Scientifically' requirements that underpin the Key Stage 1 curriculum.

> The 'Our World' section gives opportunities for pupils to **work scientifically** by:
> - Asking simple questions and recognising that they can be answered in different ways.
> - Observing closely, using simple equipment.
> - Identifying and classifying.
> - Using their observations and ideas to suggest answers to questions.

The tasks pupils complete in the **Activity Book** will help you assess pupils' understanding of the 'Seasonal Changes' section of the Year 1 Programme of Study.

For both the 'Seasonal Changes' section of the Programme of Study and the 'Working Scientifically' requirements, you can use **Classroom Assessment**.

This will allow pupils who may not have strong literacy skills to demonstrate their understanding practically and verbally.

Year 1 Science Programme of Study: SEASONAL CHANGES	KS1 Science: Working Scientifically
Observe changes across the four seasons / Observe and describe weather associated with the seasons / Observe and describe how day length varies	Observing closely, using simple equipment / Identifying and classifying / Using their observations and ideas to suggest answers to questions / Asking simple questions and recognising that they can be answered in different ways

Classroom Assessment

Classroom Assessment should be in the form of small-group work, observation and the use of open-ended questions. Try focusing on just five or six pupils in each lesson, so you get a deeper understanding of the level they're working at.

Session 1: Changing Seasons

The extension questions in this lesson plan will give you lots of opportunities to assess children's understanding of the four seasons. You can ask these during whole class teaching, giving some time for paired or group talk, or you could work with a few small groups while the class works independently. Try writing the questions out on index cards and then ask each group to pick one or two to think about, noting pupils' answers.

Initial Judgements
Notice which pupils are demonstrating an understanding of how the months and seasons make up the year. Who has first hand experience of observing the changing seasons? Who knows how this relates to things that they see in nature and the world around them?

Y1 Science PoS: Seasonal Changes	Working Scientifically
Observe changes across the four seasons ✓	Identifying and classifying ✓

Session 2: Night and Day

This lesson focuses on some tricky topics, so try observing your most able scientists. Use open-ended questions to see who has really got to grips with how the positioning of the earth and sun cause night and day. Pair these children together for the computer activity to allow you to add in some extension work and to observe how well they can use information to answer their own questions.

Prompt Questions
What have you found out so far? Where is it night time at the moment? Can you explain why? Do you have any questions that you would like to try and find out the answers to? I wonder how you could use the website to answer your question.

Session 3: What's the Weather?

By now you have had the opportunity to work with some mixed ability pairs and your most able pupils. Use this lesson to assess your least able scientists. Work with pupils in a small group on their weather report with a focus on using the correct names to describe the types of weather shown in the Activity Book. Perhaps choose a cold, snowy day in winter and discuss how the weather is different in summer. Talk about what clothes you might wear and whether you would go outside.

Intervention
You could use page 6 of the pupil Activity Book to make some weather flash cards (just photocopy and cut out). Less able children could stick these into their science books and label them as a visual reference to the different types of weather.

The suggested Follow-Up activity on weather observation enables pupils to work scientifically by observing closely using simple equipment.

Session 4: A Year in the Life of a Honeybee

Use the final lesson in the topic to fill in any gaps in your assessment. Which children can describe the differences between the four seasons? Who is able to talk about the seasons in relation to the weather, the length of day and the life of a honeybee? Talk to pupils as they fill in their worksheets and ask them to expand on their answers to give you a deeper knowledge of how well they are meeting the learning objectives.

Prompt Questions
How else might you know it is spring/summer? Why do you think the bees return to the hive in autumn? What is happening to the length of the day at that time of year? What might the weather be like? Tell me more about how you know it is winter.

Recording Pupils' Attainment

By the end of the topic, you should be confident in your judgement of which pupils in your class have met the topic's learning objectives. You should also know which pupils are yet to meet the learning objectives and which children have moved beyond the Year One Programme of Study with additional skills and knowledge.

Record pupils' attainment in the Assessment Grid on the CD-ROM. You may wish to use a traffic light system to colour-code the grid.

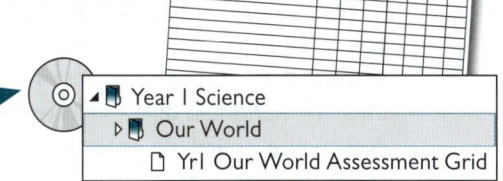

Year 1: Section Two — Plants
World of Plants

Learning Objectives:
- To name and identify a selection of different plants.
- To think about the similarities and differences between plants.
- To consider what plants might need to be able to grow.

Year 1 Science Programme of Study
"Identify and name a variety of common wild and garden plants, including deciduous and evergreen trees. Identify and describe the basic structure of a variety of common flowering plants, including trees."

Preparation: For the grouping activity, you will need to print off and cut out the cards on the CD-ROM.

For the seed planting activity, you will need either plant pots or newspaper and plastic bottles, compost, watering cans filled with water, lollipop sticks and at least one seed per child. (It's worth planting a few spares, as some will fail to germinate.) You can choose whichever seeds you like to grow, but sunflowers, broad beans and tomato plants are all fairly failsafe.

Lesson Activities

1. Show the class the slideshow of common plants from the CD-ROM and ask pupils to put up their hand if they know the name of the plant. Write down any correct answers on the white board beneath each picture.

2. Give out the cards, printed from the file on the CD-ROM, showing the different plants. In pairs or small groups, pupils should try to group the cards with a reason for why they think the plants are similar. E.g.:
"The oak and the pine are both trees."
"The rose and the tulip both have flowers."
"The carrot, the strawberry and the onion all have parts that can be eaten."

    Bring together pupils' grouping ideas, using the final slide on the PowerPoint® file as a prompt.

3. Read page 10 of the Activity Book and look at some of the ways that plants can be classified or grouped.

4. Tell the class that they are going to plant some 'secret seeds'. Show the class one of the secret seeds that they are going to plant and ask if they can guess what sort of plant it will grow into. (A handheld digital microscope that displays images on your white board is a great tool for the close observation of seeds and other plant samples, and can be quite inexpensive.)

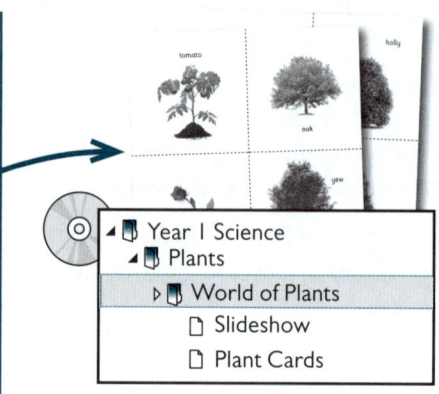

Nature Journals

This topic should be underpinned by regular observation of the local environment. Keeping nature journals, going on termly nature walks or keeping a seasonal nature table in your classroom are perfect ways for pupils to build up a portfolio of plants, flowers and trees that they can identify and name, as well as supporting learning about the seasons and animals.

Teacher Notes

The classification of plants is a complicated business and there are a lot of grey areas. For example, a banana tree is not a tree at all, but a large herb, and peanuts are not nuts, but legumes! At this stage, it is sufficient for children to be able to note the differences and similarities between plants, noticing for example whether they bear fruit, if they flower, whether they have woody stems (e.g. trees and shrubs), and any other interesting characteristics.

5. Ask the pupils to complete page 11 of the Activity Book, using the information you have shared.

6. As children finish their work in the Activity Book, they can begin to plant their seeds. Show the children how to fill their pot with compost and press it down. They can then use a pencil to make a hole a few centimetres deep in the centre of the pot, place the seed in the hole and cover it with earth. They should water the seed and place the pot somewhere warm — on a windowsill is good. They could use lollipop sticks to add a name label to the pot.

Over the coming weeks, children will observe their seeds as they sprout and grow. A nice way to do this is to keep a plant diary, asking pupils to draw pictures every few days of what their plant looks like (alternatively they could take photographs). They could observe changes using a magnifying glass and take measurements using a ruler. The plants will need regular watering, and will eventually need repotting and moving outside.

After a few weeks, children might start to be able to identify which plant their seed is growing into, especially as they begin to flower or fruit.

Teacher Notes
Biodegradable pots can be made from newspaper that has been moulded around a plastic bottle. These pots can then be planted in the ground, and will decompose.

Extension Ideas
Early finishers can think about what their seeds will need to grow. At first they will just need somewhere warm, and plenty of water. But as they grow they will also need light to make food, and maybe protection from pests that might want to eat them.

Plenary Questions

1. What do we need to do to make sure our seeds grow?
2. Roses, daffodils and geraniums are all flowering plants that lots of people like to grow in their gardens. What other flowers might you find in a garden?
3. Trees are a type of plant with woody stems. Oak and pine are two types of tree. Can anyone name any more?

Follow-Up Ideas

1. Your growing plants will provide a good opportunity for learning to accurately measure with a ruler. At the end of the project you could plot these measurements as a graph and look at when the most and least growth occurred.

2. Read 'The Tiny Seed' by Eric Carle. Discuss what seeds need in order to survive and some of the threats that they face. Show pupils the video below on how dandelion seeds are carried by the wind:
www.bbc.co.uk/education/clips/zhrb4wx
Pupils could write their own story or poem about the journey of a dandelion seed.

3. Read 'Handa's Surprise' by Eileen Browne and bring in some of the fruits from Handa's basket (banana, guava, orange, mango, pineapple, avocado, passion fruit and tangerine). Allow children to taste some of the fruits and then closely examine the different seeds. Which are the same and which are different? Which has the smallest seeds? Which has the biggest? Where in the world do these fruits grow? Why couldn't they grow in the UK?

Flowering Plants

> **Learning Objectives:**
> - To explore the structure of flowering plants by observing similarities and differences.
> - To understand that different species of flowering plant can be identified by their flowers.
> - To learn the names of some common flowering plants.
>
> **Year 1 Science Programme of Study**
> "Identify and name a variety of common wild and garden plants. Identify and describe the basic structure of a variety of common flowering plants."

Preparation: *Bring in a collection of potted flowering plants (which you don't mind being pulled apart!). If possible, include a plant that grows from a bulb. Also provide a set of magnifying glasses. Be aware that some plants may be poisonous or more likely to cause allergic reactions — these are best avoided.*

Lesson Activities

1. Divide a selection of flowering plants around the classroom, with magnifying glasses.

2. In pairs, children should visit a selection of the plants in turn, studying each plant with a magnifying glass. Encourage them to SEE, SNIFF and FEEL each plant carefully, talking about their observations.

3. Gather the children back together and select a few interesting plants, asking children to share their observations about each one with the class.

4. Give 2 minutes of paired talking time to discuss the following questions:

   a. "How are some of the plants <u>different</u> from each other?"

   b. "What do all of these plants have <u>in common</u>?"

5. Read page 12 of the Activity Book together. Discuss what features all flowering plants have in common, with reference to the plants you brought in.

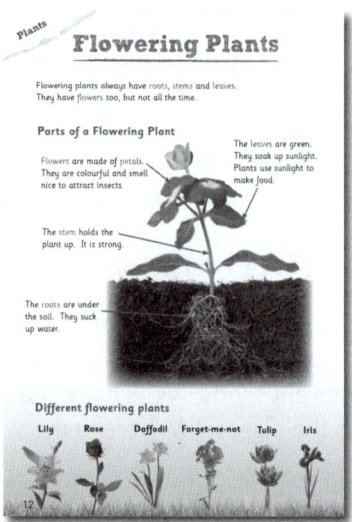

Teacher Notes

Flowers and Petals
Pupils may notice that some plants have many small flowers and others have just one large flower. They may comment on the colour, size, smell and number of petals on each flower. Some flowers (like the petunia) have 'fused' petals where the whole flower is one big petal. Others (like the dandelion) have so many tiny petals that you can't count them!

Leaves
Leaves come in all sorts of shapes and sizes — encourage children to describe them using appropriate vocabulary, e.g. long, rounded, with 'leaflets' or 'teeth'. Point out the singular 'leaf' and plural 'leaves'.

Stems
Ask pupils to look carefully at a hairy stem and a smooth stem — can they tell the difference? Some stems may have thorns — be careful! These are to protect the plant.

Roots
If roots have not been seen on all the plant examples, pull a plant from its pot to uncover the roots. Make sure children are clear that ALL plants have roots — you just don't often see them because they are underground.

Bulbs
Some plants grow from a bulb — the roots come out of the bottom and the stem comes out of the top. Show children a real bulb if possible — an onion would do!

Year 1: Section Two — Plants

6. Ask pupils to work through page 13 of the Activity Book.

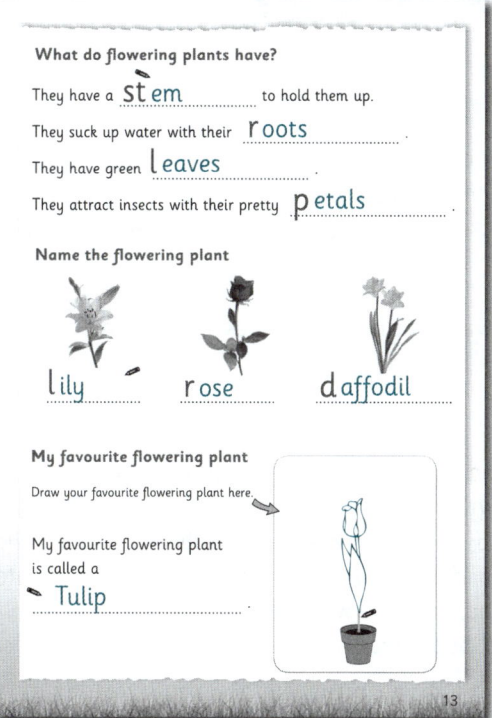

Extension Questions

"Have you ever seen flowers on trees?"
Yes — flowers on trees are called <u>blossom</u>. You see blossom in the springtime on trees that grow fruit. When the petals fall off, the bit of flower that's left grows into a fruit in the summer!

"Are there any plants that don't have flowers?"
Yes — ferns and mosses, and also coniferous trees (ones that have cones like pine trees). Children might name fungi — it's true that they don't have flowers but they aren't technically plants as they're not green and don't photosynthesise to make food. Children might also name vegetables, but plants that produce vegetables will normally produce flowers as well — we just aren't used to seeing them!

Extension Activity

Ask early finishers to carefully sketch and colour a plant of their choice from the selection. Encourage them to copy the shape of the petals and leaves accurately so that the type of plant can be identified. Show each sketch to the class to see if they can spot which plant it is. A display could be made of these sketches, perhaps alongside photographs of the real plants.

7. Pupils can now see if they can identify any of the plants in the collection you have brought in. They can use the images from the Activity Book to help with this, or you may like to provide books to help with other plants. This website is also useful for exploring and identifying different flowers: www.mywildflowers.com/identify.asp

Plenary Questions

1. What do all flowering plants have in common?
2. Can you name any flowering plants?
3. What have you learned about each part of a flowering plant?

Follow-Up Ideas

1. Ask pupils to design a new type of flowering plant (see the worksheet on the CD-ROM). It must have the structure of a flowering plant (i.e. roots, stem, leaves, flower) and must be realistic, but can be imaginative. Children should try to use some of the flower or leaf shapes that they have seen on real plants. They should give their plant a name and briefly describe it.

2. Make your own class garden or vase of flowers. Pupils can draw round the templates on the CD-ROM onto coloured tissue paper for the leaves and petals, then cut them out and stick them around a green pipe cleaner with PVA glue. To be really accurate, add string for roots! Each child can make their own flowering plant to add to the display. Alternatively, home-made flowers can make excellent presents.

3. Children could investigate unusual flowers from around the world using this resource:
10mosttoday.com/10-most-unusual-flowers-in-the-world

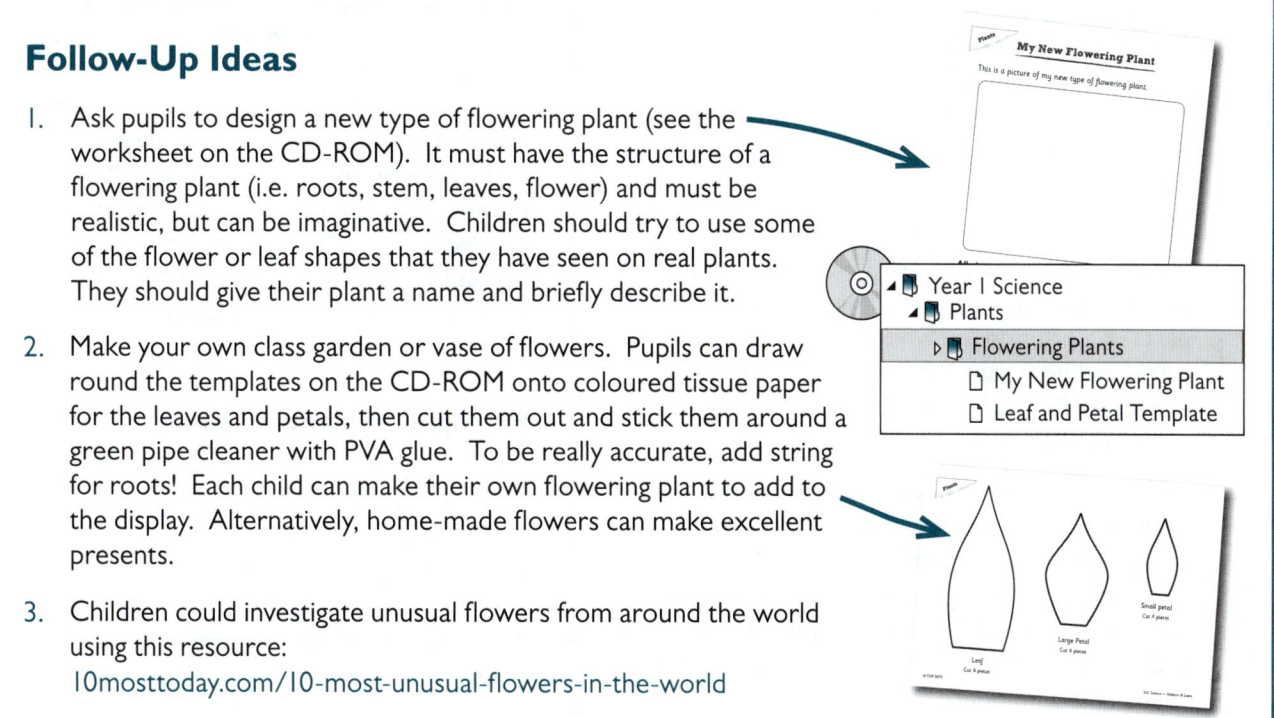

Year 1: Section Two — Plants

Plants We Eat

Learning Objectives:
- To name a range of edible plants including fruits, vegetables and herbs.
- To identify the different parts of a plant and know that some parts can be safely eaten.

Year 1 Science Programme of Study
"Identify and describe the basic structure of a variety of common flowering plants. Identify and name a variety of common wild and garden plants."

Preparation: *For this lesson you will need a selection of plant foods for the class to taste, including at least one food from each part of the plant (there are some suggestions below). If possible, provide an example of the whole plant or food, and then some small prepared samples that have been chopped or cooked if appropriate. Children should wash their hands in soapy water before beginning and should have access to napkins and water during the tasting session. You will need to be aware of any allergies that pupils may have before doing the tasting activity.*

Lesson Activities

1. Sit the class in a circle and explain that they are going to be learning about plants that can be eaten (plants that are 'edible'). Recap the different parts of a plant (roots, stem, leaves, fruit, flowers, seeds, bulb) and show these on the whiteboard. Tell the children that they will be tasting each of these different parts today, but from different plants.

2. Establish some ground rules for tasting the foods (see the Tasting Etiquette notes on the right) and then introduce one food at a time.

3. First show the whole plant, or as much of it as possible (you could show a photo if it comes from a tree or large bush). Ask the children if they know what plant it is and which part of it they can eat. Pass it around the circle for the children to look at, touch and smell (you might want to cut a section in half beforehand).

4. Next pass round a container with some prepared pieces of the food in it. Explain which part of the plant they are eating (refer to the parts of a plant on the white board), what it is called and how you have prepared it (some might be raw and whole, others might have been cut into chunks or cooked).

5. After everyone has tasted a sample of each plant, ask pupils to talk in pairs about which were their favourites and any that they didn't like. Share the findings as a class and note which were the most popular and unpopular foods. Did the parts of the plants they came from have anything in common?

Safety First!

At the beginning of the lesson it will be important to give a health and safety reminder to the class. While some plants provide delicious foods, not all plants are safe to eat. Some members of the potato family are very poisonous, and some berries that are safe for birds to eat can make us very sick. Children should always check with an adult before eating any plants that they find.

Tasting Etiquette

Before starting a tasting activity it is a good idea to establish some etiquette. Ensure children wash their hands first, provide napkins and water, and ask children to spit any food they don't like into a napkin and then put it in the bin. Remind pupils not to shout out if they don't like something, as it might put others off trying, and reassure them that you need to try new foods a few times before you get used to them. The key today is to try as many as possible and there will be time at the end to share which ones we liked and disliked.

Examples of plants to eat

Seeds – sunflower seeds, chickpeas, beans.
Flowers – broccoli, cauliflower, chive flowers.
Fruits – pepper, cucumber, melon.
Stems – celery, asparagus, rhubarb.
Leaves – spinach, mint, basil.
Roots – carrots, beetroot, sweet potato.
Bulbs – fennel, leek, onion.

6. Ask the children to complete the worksheet from the CD-ROM. They should record some of the foods that they tasted, by drawing the plant, labelling which part of the plant they ate, whether or not they liked it and why.

7. Read pages 14-15 of the Activity Book together and recap what has been learned this lesson. Ask pupils to complete the activities on these pages.

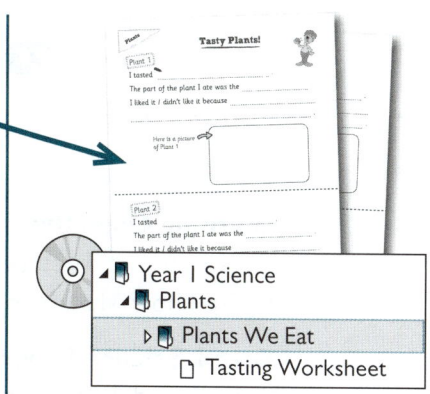

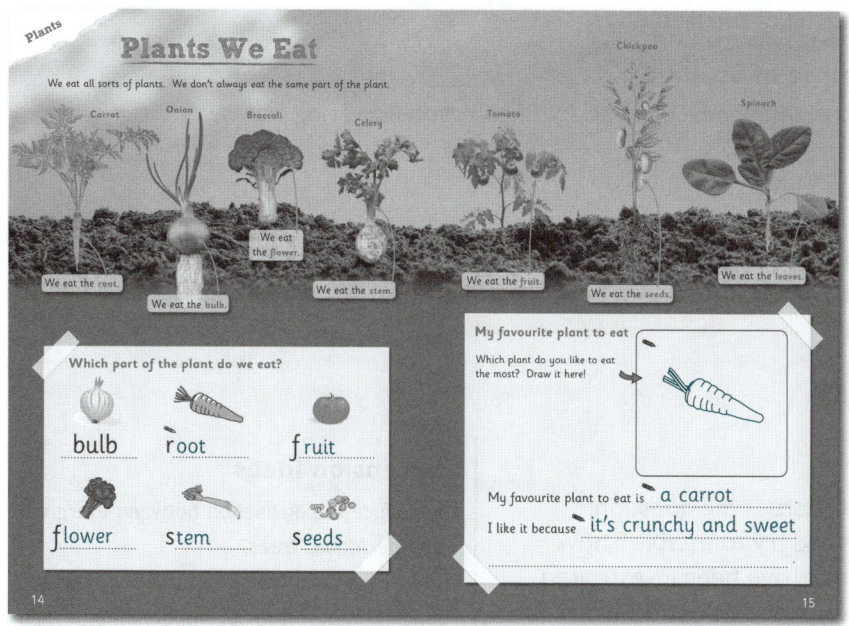

Extension Ideas

Ask early finishers to look at the list of plant parts again and think of any other foods that come from each part. Can they come up with a different food for each plant part?

Plenary Questions

1. What different parts of plants have we tasted today?

2. Does anyone grow fruit or vegetables in their gardens? What do you grow? Which part of the plant do you eat?

3. What is it important to remember before you eat a plant that is growing in your garden or in the wild?

Follow-Up Ideas

1. This lesson provides a good springboard into a wider discussion about healthy eating. You could look at different food groups and talk about the importance of eating at least 5 different servings of fruit and vegetables each day. Children might like to plan a meal using their favourite fruits and vegetables, or could make fruit and veg smoothies from their favourite plants they ate in the tasting activity.

2. Cooking vegetable samosas is a good way to introduce basic chopping and cooking skills and can be done in small groups.

3. Leave some celery stalks (with leaves on) sitting in coloured water and see the colour travel up the stalks and into the leaves. This is a good way of demonstrating one of the functions of a plant's stem. There are more details here:
   www.education.com/activity/article/celery_stick_science_first/

4. In an art lesson you could have a go at making some vegetable dyes — carrot, red cabbage, onion skins and turmeric work well. Pupils can try painting with them or dying scraps of fabric. Here are some instructions on making vegetable dyes to colour T-shirts:
   www.planet-science.com/categories/experiments/chemistry-chaos/2012/06/dye-your-clothes-with-food.aspx

Parts of a Tree

Learning Objectives:
- To name and describe the different parts of a tree.
- To know what job each part of the tree does.

Year 1 Science Programme of Study
"Identify and describe the basic structure of a variety of common flowering plants, including trees."

Preparation: For this lesson you will need a range of art materials for the class to make their own tree art. These may include sugar paper, brown paper bags, paint, old soft drinks bottles, tissue paper, glue and scissors.

Lesson Activities

1. Ask the children to talk in pairs and discuss the question, "What is a tree?" Gather answers and try to establish how trees differ from the other plants that have been investigated so far in this section.

2. Show a selection of photos of trees. This is a fantastic webpage, showing sixteen of the most magnificent trees in the world: www.boredpanda.com/most-beautiful-trees

3. Ask pupils to notice what features all of the trees have. Using their knowledge of plants, can they guess what job each part of the tree does?

4. Read page 16 of the Activity Book together. Then look at a few of the photographs again and ask the class to spot the features on each tree and discuss what they do. Notice how some of the trees grow tall and thin, while others are low and wide. Why could that be?

5. Ask pupils to complete page 17 of the Activity Book:

Extension Ideas

Introduce the distinction between evergreen *and* deciduous *trees.*

Evergreen trees, or just 'evergreens', often grow up into a triangle shape and lose their leaves gradually through the year. Probably the best known example is a fir — children may recognise this as a type of Christmas tree. Their seeds grow in cones and their leaves are long and thin and are sometimes called needles.

Deciduous trees lose their leaves in autumn and stop growing in winter.
They tend to grow out into a rounder shape and their branches spread out wide. Their seeds are either inside fruits or nuts and their leaves are usually big and flat. Deciduous trees will be covered more in the next session.

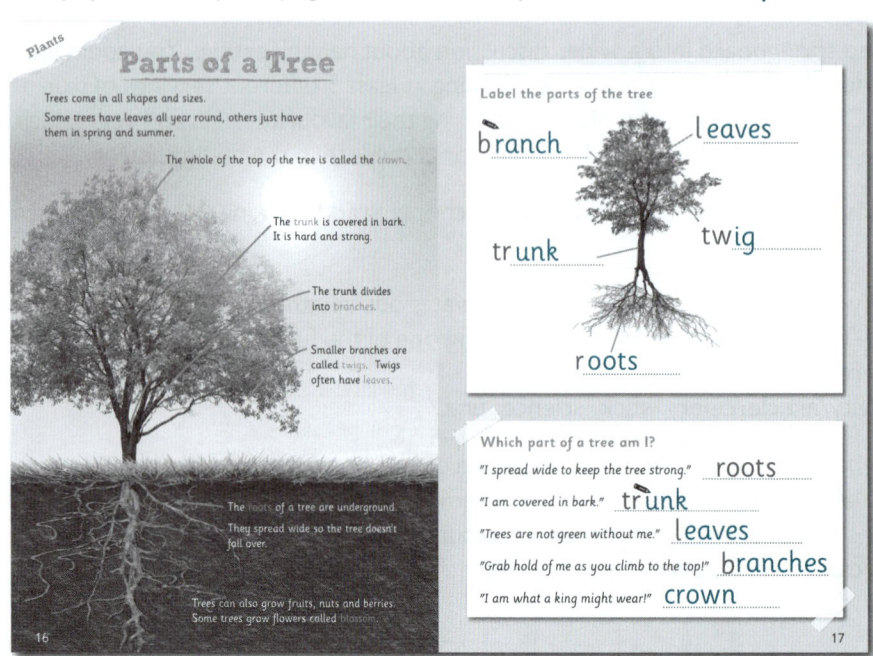

Year 1: Section Two — Plants

6. Now ask the children to make some tree art with a focus on including the important features: roots, trunk, branches, twigs, leaves and crown. They can do this in several ways — you may wish to model one way and provide a limited number of resources, or you could show the class a few different options and let them choose.

   Below are some suggestions with links to further instructions.

   a. Use brown paper and tissue paper to make a tree sculpture: craftsbyamanda.com/paper-bag-tree

   b. Hand print trees are effective:
      www.craftymorning.com/kids-handprint-fall-tree-craft

   c. You could use real leaves to print with:
      www.firstpalette.com/Craft_themes/Nature/Leaf_Prints_Tree/Leaf_Prints_Tree.html

   d. You could even use the bottom of a water bottle to create the effect of blossom:
      alphamom.com/family-fun/holidays/cherry-blossom-art-from-a-recycled-soda-bottle

Extension Ideas

Investigate how pine cones can be used to predict the weather! Place some pine cones on the windowsill. When the weather is dry, the pine cones will open up to allow the wind to blow their seeds away. When the weather becomes more humid, they close up to protect their seeds — so if the pine cones are closed, it is probably going to rain.

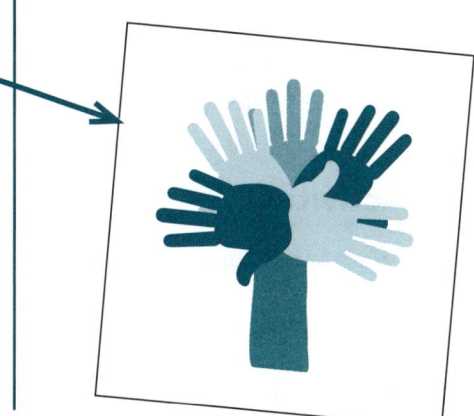

Plenary Questions

1. Share examples of class tree art. Can we clearly see each feature? Do we think it is a deciduous or evergreen tree?

2. Does anyone know the names of any trees? (Note these down for next lesson.)

3. Why might trees in hot dry countries need deep roots?

Follow-Up Ideas

1. It would be great to arrange a visit to a local forest or wooded area to have a look at some real trees and identify their different parts. You can also use this trip as a chance to collect leaves for the next lesson.

2. Ask the children whether they have ever climbed a tree. Do they have any photographs of them climbing trees, which they could bring in to add to your plants display? Can they identify the tree that they climbed? Discuss what makes climbing trees easier or harder in relation to the parts of a tree (e.g. low, wide branches to hold onto).

3. Look at how paper is made from trees and the importance of recycling paper and buying recycled products such as toilet roll. You could have a go at making your own recycled paper, using the instructions here: tinkerlab.com/how-to-make-paper

4. Discuss how many of the materials and products that we use come from trees. As well as paper, there is wooden furniture, rubber, fruits and nuts. Many others are shown in the infographic at the bottom of this webpage: www.idahoforests.org/wood_you.htm

Year 1: Section Two — Plants

Deciduous Trees

Learning Objectives:
- To explore the structure of leaves by observing similarities and differences.
- To understand that different species of tree can be identified by their leaves and seeds.
- To learn the names of some common deciduous trees.

Year 1 Science Programme of Study
"Identify and name a variety of common deciduous trees. Identify and describe the basic structure of a variety of common trees."

Preparation: Take the children to a wooded area to collect some leaves from deciduous trees. Encourage pupils to gather leaves of different shapes and sizes, and different species of tree. Alternatively, ask pupils to gather some leaves over a weekend and bring them in.

Lesson Activities

1. Split the class into groups. Divide out the leaves, ensuring each group has a variety of different types of leaf. Ask pupils to sort the leaves into piles of leaves that they think look similar. They can then explain their groups to the rest of the class.

2. Read the top of pages 18-19 of the Activity Book together.

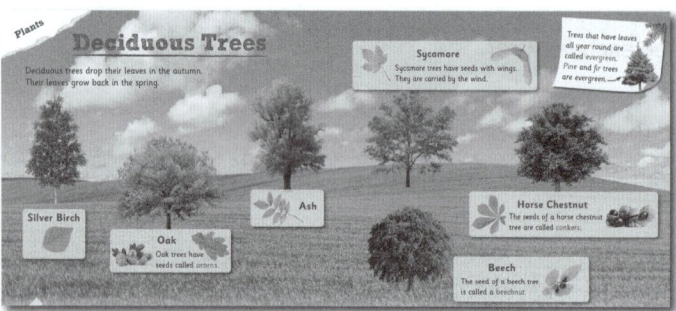

3. Recap understanding of **seasons** (pages 4-5). Discuss what the season is now, how this relates to the colour of the leaves, and whether the leaves are on the ground or still on the trees. Discuss the fact that only deciduous trees drop all their leaves in autumn. Some trees (coniferous or evergreen) lose their leaves gradually throughout the year, and so have leaves all year round. Also recap what the seeds of plants are for.

4. Pupils should now use the information on these pages to identify which tree their leaves come from. They can then arrange their leaves according to which tree they come from. For leaves that don't appear in the Activity Book, they could visit this website:
www.woodlands.co.uk/blog/tree-identification

Extension Ideas

Introduce pupils to some of these general features of leaves. Pupils can then continue classifying according to these particular features, e.g. 'toothed'/'untoothed'; 'lobed'/'unlobed'.

Leaflets
*Pupils may notice that some leaves (e.g. ash and horse chestnut leaves) look like they are made up of smaller leaves. These are called **leaflets**.*

Teeth
*The ridges round the outside of some leaves are called **teeth**. Elicit why they might be called teeth. (Other things are said to have teeth, like saws and combs.) Even ridges that are wide apart, like those on a sycamore leaf, are still called teeth. Pupils could observe the teeth on some leaves using a magnifying glass. They may then be able to notice that some leaves (e.g. most elm leaves) are **doubly toothed** — they have teeth on teeth.*

Lobes
*Ask pupils what the round bits of an oak leaf might be called. Encourage imaginative responses. In fact they're called **lobes** — like ear lobes.*

Veins
*Ask pupils to look at their wrists. Can they see any blood vessels? Do any of the leaves have something similar? They're called **veins** too!*

Extension Question

"Why do you think some trees lose their leaves in the autumn?"
Leaves can get damaged in the cold weather. Trees can reabsorb some of the nutrients in their leaves and keep them stored for later.

5. Ask pupils to make **leaf rubs** of some their leaves, and label them with the tree they're from.

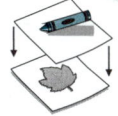

6. Ask pupils to work through the activities on pages 18-19 of the Activity Book:

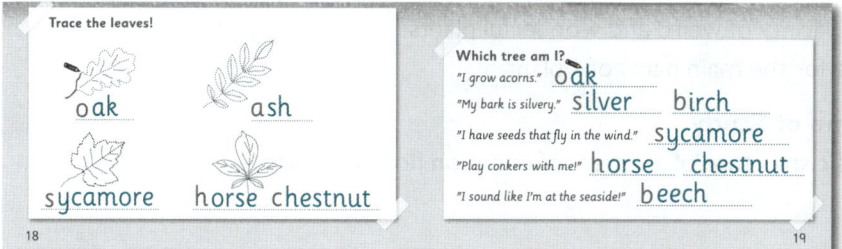

Phonics & Spelling Links

Use the words 'beech', 'birch' and 'chestnut' when teaching the 'ch' sound.

The words 'conker', 'acorn' and 'sycamore' are examples of 'c' pronounced as /k/.

Teacher Notes

Acorns, conkers and beechnuts are actually nuts, rather than seeds. This means they're a sort of hard fruit with the seed(s) inside.

Extension Activity

Ask early finishers to make up their own sentences for "Which tree am I?" — either orally (in pairs), or on paper. Encourage them to look to a feature of the tree or its name for inspiration.

Plenary Questions

1. What have we learned about trees today? Can anyone name any?
   Other common deciduous trees found in Britain are elm, willow, alder, lime, cherry and rowan.

2. What new word have we learned today, beginning with 'd'? What does it mean?

3. What can help us to identify a tree (tell us what type of tree it is)?

Follow-Up Ideas

1. Ask pupils to find a tree near their home or school that they particularly like, and draw the tree. If possible, ask them to collect a leaf from the tree. They can then draw the leaf, and try to identify the species of tree.

2. Pupils may like to write a poem about their tree. They could also observe the changes of their tree over time — and keep a log of what they observe.

3. Sycamore leaves often have black spots from an infection called Tar Spot. Each pupil has to find a leaf with a black spot. They then arrange themselves in order of number of spots on their leaf. If there is a number missing, they can try to find a leaf with the required number of spots.

   Pupils can then make sums with the spotted leaves, using stems to create '+', '−' and '=' signs.

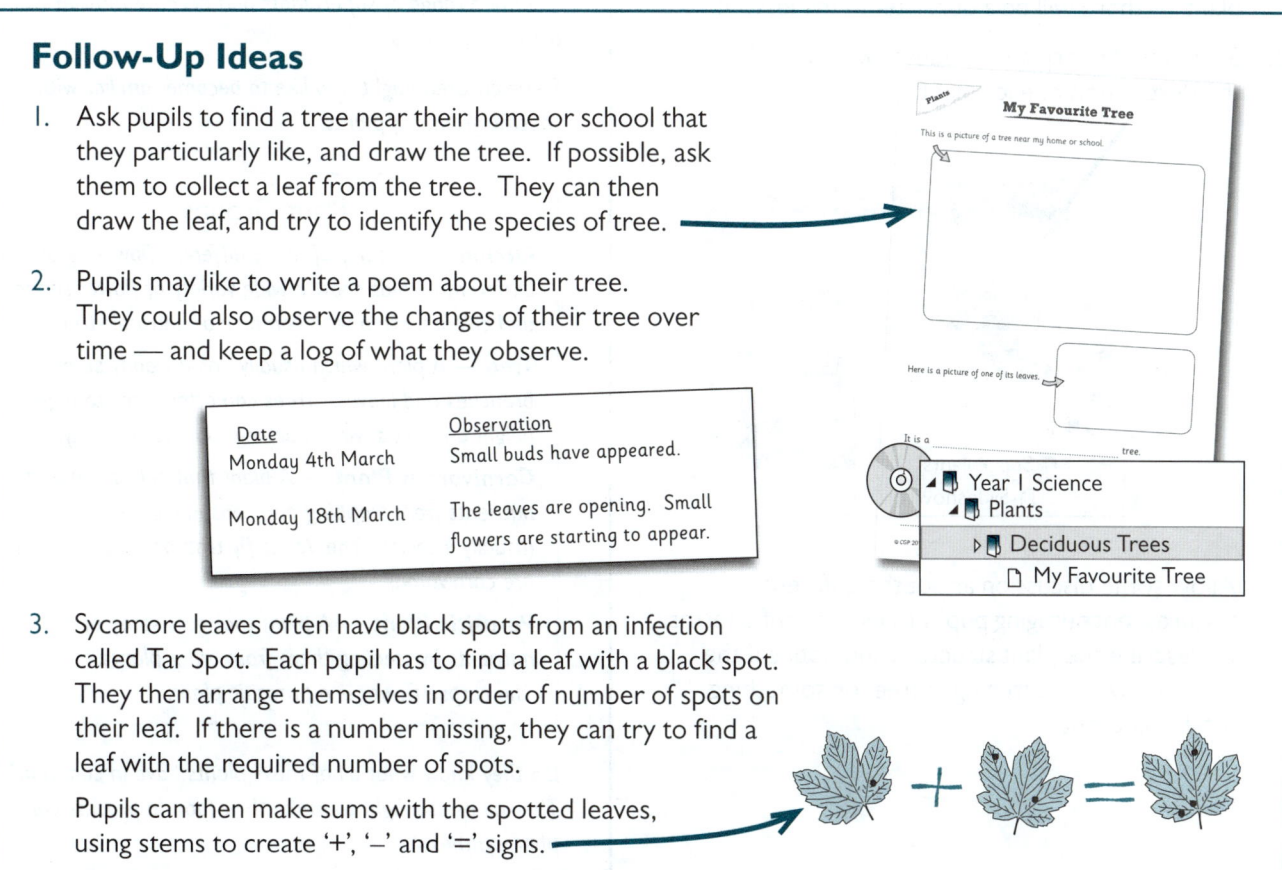

Year 1: Section Two — Plants

Superplants!

'Superplants!' is a **synoptic topic** for the Plants section. It builds on the concepts introduced in the preceding sessions and applies them to a real-world context.

Learning Objectives:
- To recognise and name a variety of weird and wonderful plants.
- To use the scientific name for the main parts of a plant.

Year 1 Science Programme of Study
"Identify and describe the basic structure of a variety of common flowering plants, including trees."

Preparation: For this lesson you will need the 'Superplants!' slideshow and the list of descriptions to go with it. You will also need to print and laminate a set of 'Superplants!' cards (one set should be enough, but if you have a large class you may require some duplicates).

It would also be helpful for children to have access to a range of suitable reading material about plants, so that they can research further examples or look up additional information with some support.

Lesson Activities

1. Explain to the class that today they are going to be identifying a selection of weird and wonderful 'superplants'. They will need to take careful notice of the different features of each plant — there will be a quiz later in the lesson!

2. Show the 'Superplants!' slideshow and read out the description of each plant.

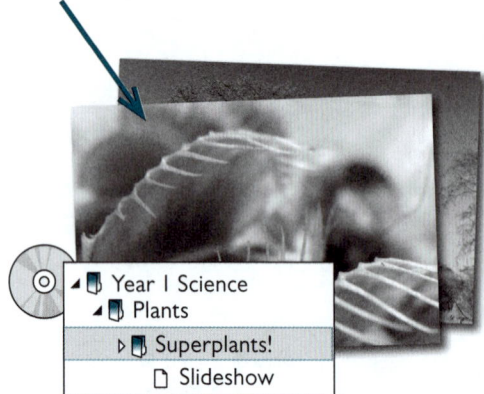

Allow some discussion about the different features, encouraging pupils to use scientific terms to describe the plant structure and noting if the plant is flowering, fruiting, a tree, or something totally different.

Teacher Notes

For most pupils it will be sufficient to learn to name and identify a range of superplants and become familiar with their key features.

Some children might also like to become familiar with specific groups of plants:

Plant Groups

Orchid — *A family of many different flowering plants. Different orchids show a wide variety of flower shapes and colours, often with complex or unusual structures.*

Tree — *A plant which usually has a woody stem, branches and leaves. Trees can often grow to a great height and need wide-reaching roots for stability.*

Carnivorous Plant — *A plant that gets some of its nutrients from trapping and consuming animals (usually insects). The Venus fly trap and pitcher plant are carnivorous.*

Parasitic Plant — *A plant that gets some of its nutrients by stealing them from other plants. The corpse flower is a parasitic plant.*

Do they know what all of these plants have in common? They all use sunlight to make their food (a process called photosynthesis).

3. Read page 20 of the Activity Book together.
   Ask the children to complete page 21 independently.

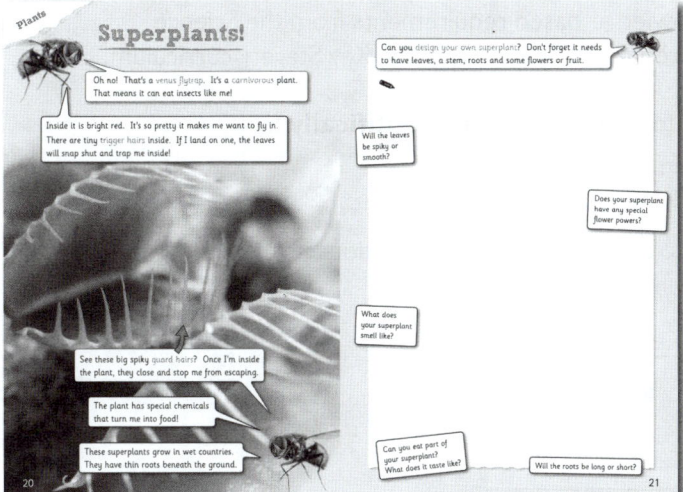

4. Pupils should now be familiar with the 10 superplants and their features. Split the class into groups of 2 or 3 and give each group a superplant card printed from the CD-ROM, which they must keep hidden from the rest of the class (putting them in envelopes will make this easier). Pupils will now work together to devise a series of clues, which they will later read to the rest of the class, who will try to guess which superplant is being described.

5. Quiz Time! Divide the class into two teams and make a space for the Quizmasters at the front. Ask each group to take a turn at being Quizmasters — they will read out their clues and the first team to guess which plant is being described wins a point.

Teacher Notes

Encourage pupils to incorporate some of the extreme features they have learned about into their own superplants — for example, nasty smells, enormous coloured flowers, toxic poisons and the ability to grow in difficult places. Pupils' superplants can be as outlandish as they like, but you should remind them to include the important parts of the plant structure. More able children might like to think about how each feature is useful to the plant's survival — for example, plants in very dry places tend to have long, deep roots to help them collect water and carnivorous plants usually have some kind of trap.

Extension Ideas

Once pupils have designed their superplant, they could have a go at collaging, painting or junk modelling their design, to bring their plants to life.

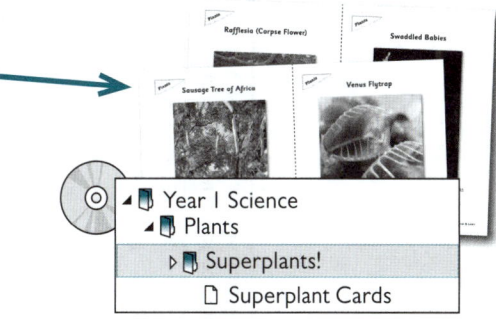

Extension Ideas

You might like to give more able groups one or two words that they cannot use in their description to add more of a challenge. For example, they might not be able to use the word 'sausage' for the sausage tree, or 'starfish' for starfish flower.

Plenary Questions

1. Which superplant would you least like to touch?
2. Which superplant would you grow in your garden?
3. Can anyone name all 10 superplants?

Follow-Up Ideas

1. There are lots more superplants to investigate around the world. Why not choose a country or continent and learn about it in some more detail? You could investigate the food, culture and other wildlife, as well as the plants that grow there.

2. You could find out how even common plants can have 'superpowers' — like cleaning the air for us. There is some information here:
   www.kidsgardening.org/lesson-plans-indoor-greening
   Choose some plants to create an indoor garden in your classroom, and encourage children to help take care of them.

3. You could read the story of Jack and the Beanstalk, possibly the most famous superplant of all. Children could write their own versions of Jack and the Superplant, where they receive magic beans that grow into one of the plants that they have learned about.

Year 1: Section Two — Plants

Notes on Assessment (Plants)

You'll need to assess pupils' understanding of both the knowledge-based requirements from the Science Programme of Study and the 'Working Scientifically' requirements that underpin the Key Stage 1 curriculum.

> The 'Plants' section gives opportunities for pupils to **work scientifically** by:
> - Observing closely, using simple equipment.
> - Identifying and classifying plants.
> - Using their observations and ideas to suggest answers to questions.

The tasks pupils complete in the **Activity Book** will help you assess pupils' understanding of the 'Plants' section of the Year 1 Programme of Study.

Year 1 Science Programme of Study: PLANTS	KS1 Science: Working Scientifically
Identify and name a variety of common wild and garden plants / Identify and name a variety of common deciduous and evergreen trees / Identify and describe the basic structure of a variety of common flowering plants / Identify and describe the basic structure of a variety of common trees	Observing closely, using simple equipment / Identifying and classifying / Using their observations and ideas to suggest answers to questions

For both the 'Plants' section of the Programme of Study and the 'Working Scientifically' requirements, you can use **Classroom Assessment**.

This will allow pupils who may not have strong literacy skills to demonstrate their understanding practically and verbally.

Classroom Assessment

Classroom Assessment should be in the form of small-group work, observation and the use of open-ended questions. Try focusing on just five or six pupils in each lesson, so you get a deeper understanding of the level they're working at.

Session 1: World of Plants

Choose one group to work with during the grouping activity. Stand back and observe their suggestions for how they could group together the plant cards. Which pupils in the group are able to independently identify similarities between some of the plants? Who is making sound suggestions for how they could be classified?

Prompt Questions
Who can spot two plants that are similar in some way? Can you explain your answer to me?
I wonder if anyone can spot a plant that's similar to this one... Why do you think that?

Session 2: Flowering Plants

Choose several pairs to shadow during the observation activity. Notice how they engage with the plants and use the magnifying glasses. Which pupils are looking carefully at the plants and using the magnifying glasses correctly? Who is using all of their senses to explore and investigate the plant structures?

Prompt Questions
What have you noticed about that plant? Tell me more.
I wonder if anyone can name any parts of the plant...

Session 3: Plants We Eat

Use the beginning of this lesson to find out which children have consolidated their knowledge of the different parts of a plant. Note down which children are confidently using scientific language to describe plants and which can recognise and name some of the edible plants. Which children have gaps in their knowledge? Try to focus on this group during the lesson and work with them to move towards describing the basic structure of plants.

Intervention
Some children may benefit from making up some actions for each part of the plant.

Session 4: Parts of a Tree

During the class discussion make a note of any children who demonstrate good understanding of the question 'What is a tree?'. Which children use their existing knowledge of plants to make sensible suggestions about the parts of a tree and their functions? When children are making their tree sculpture or painting, choose a few children to observe. Are they using their scientific knowledge to inform their artwork?

Prompt Questions
Tell me about your tree. I wonder what this bit here is...
Can you explain what that part of the tree does?

Session 5: Deciduous Trees

Use this lesson to focus on which pupils are developing their observation skills and, specifically, who can then use their observations to answer a question by matching leaves to the correct trees. Choose a mixed ability group to observe. You might like to give this group access to magnifying glasses and digital microscopes, so that you can assess their ability to observe closely using equipment.

Intervention
This type of group activity provides an opportunity to do some focused teaching on the use of magnifying glasses and microscopes with those pupils who need some support.

Session 6: Superplants!

This synoptic session is a great chance to assess what pupils have learned in the Plants section. Try and work with pupils whose progress you are unsure of. Use some of the questions below to complete your assessment grid. You might also choose to spend some time with your more able scientists. Consider grouping them together and then work with them on the extension activities, noting which pupils have met or exceeded the learning objectives.

Prompt Questions
Can you describe your superplant to me?
What job do you think this part of the plant does?

Recording Pupils' Attainment

By the end of the topic, you should be confident in your judgement of which pupils in your class have met the topic's learning objectives. You should also know which pupils are yet to meet the learning objectives and which children have moved beyond the Year One Programme of Study with additional skills and knowledge.

Record pupils' attainment in the Assessment Grid on the CD-ROM. You may wish to use a traffic light system to colour-code the grid.

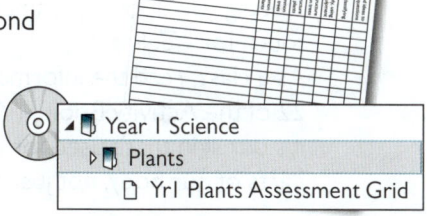

Year 1: Section Three — Animals
The Human Body

Learning Objectives:
- To name and label the main parts of the human body.
- To identify the body part that is used for each of our five senses.

Year 1 Science Programme of Study
"Identify, name, draw and label the basic parts of the human body and say which part of the body is associated with each sense."

Preparation: You will need large pieces of paper, big enough to draw round the outline of a child's body. (You may need to tape several sheets of paper together.)

Lesson Activities

1. Discuss the fact that people (elicit or introduce the word 'humans' to use from now on) come in all different shapes and sizes, but that we all have the same body parts. Sensitivity will be required when dealing with any disabilities, different skin colour, sizes, etc. Split the class into small groups and ask them to think of five things that their bodies all have in common. Take feedback from the groups and record their ideas as a class.

2. Read the top half of page 22 of the Activity Book together.

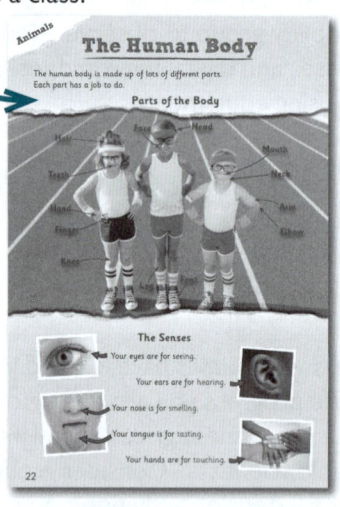

3. Reinforce the fact that humans are animals rather than plants. Discuss how the human body is similar to and different from the bodies of other types of animal. Are we more like some animals than others? You may wish to introduce the term 'mammals', which will be covered in more depth in the next session.

4. Discuss the body parts labelled in the Activity Book and ask the children to identify each part on themselves.

5. Give each group a large piece of paper and ask them to draw round the outline of one child lying down on the paper. They can then use the vocabulary from the Activity Book to draw in and label the body parts.

6. Introduce the term 'senses', i.e. the five main ways that we find out about the world around us. Ask the children to suggest what our five senses are — sight (they will likely say "seeing" or "looking"), smell, hearing/listening, taste and touch (or "feeling").
As a class, read the information on the bottom half of page 22 of the Activity Book. (You may want to point out that it's our skin that's used for touching — we can feel with all parts of our body, not just our hands.)

Phonics & Spelling Links

Use the words 'face' and 'nose' when teaching the split digraphs 'a-e' and 'o-e'.

Use the words 'teeth' and 'knee' as examples of the 'ee' sound.

Extension Question

"Can you label any other body parts?"
Encourage pupils to use phonic strategies to spell the names of these additional body parts.

Extension Question

"How are our bodies different from some other animals?"
- "Humans only have two legs."
  However, like many other animals, we have four limbs. Some other animals can also stand upright on their hind limbs, e.g. squirrels and kangaroos.
- "Humans don't have tails."
  Explain that we do have a 'tailbone' (the 'coccyx') at the base of our spine.
- "Humans don't have horns / hooves / tusks."
  Horns and hooves are made out of keratin, which makes them similar to human nails. Tusks are just teeth that stick out a very long way!
- "Some animals can breathe underwater."
  Animals such as fish have gills that they use to take oxygen out of the water. Humans (and even some other animals that live in the water, such as dolphins) have lungs, which they use to take oxygen from the air.

7. Ask pupils to work through page 23 of the Activity Book.

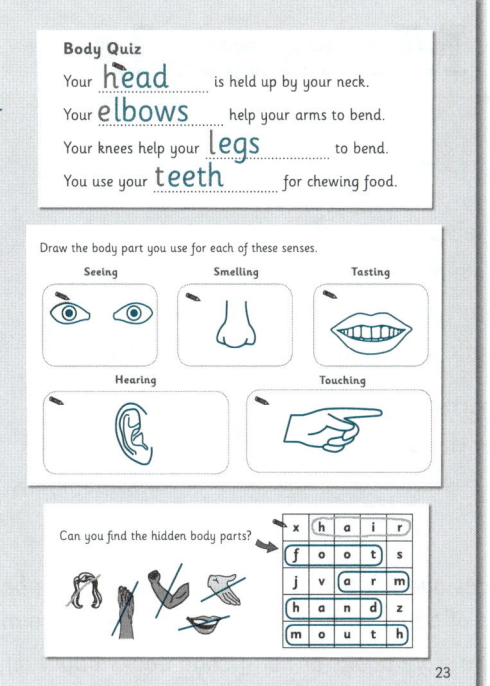

Extension Activity

Ask early finishers to have a go at making up their own wordsearches on squared paper.

Plenary Questions

1. Can you point to your head, elbow, tongue, etc.?
2. Which part of the body do we use to see / smell / touch / hear / taste?

Follow-Up Ideas

1. Sing "Head, Shoulders, Knees and Toes" — you could ask the children to suggest adaptations to the song using different body parts (e.g. "Hair, elbows, legs and hands..."). Search online for videos of other songs about body parts.

2. Learn the names of the parts of the body in different languages. Children who can speak a language other than English could teach their classmates. These new names could be incorporated into one of the songs you have learnt.

3. Take the children outside to complete some sensory activities. You can use the worksheet on the CD-ROM as a guide.

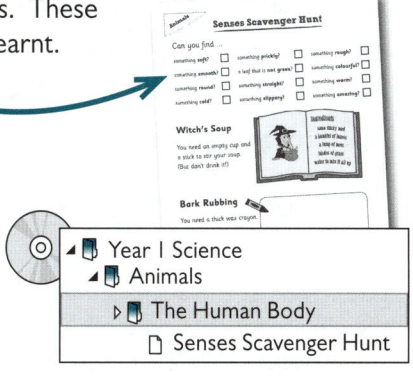

4. Carry out some tests or games where one of the senses is impaired, for example:
   a. feeling objects while blindfolded and guessing what they are,
   b. leading a blindfolded partner around a simple obstacle course or outdoor area, focusing on 'being their eyes' and giving clear instructions,
   c. taste tests, e.g. different types of fruit or different flavours of crisps (be aware of allergies),
   d. pointing to pictures of animals, musical instruments, etc. when listening to recorded sounds,
   e. wearing headphones/earmuffs and lipreading a partner's speech,
   f. playing games such as "Grandma's Footsteps", which rely on pin-pointing sounds,
   g. have pots of 'mystery smells' (e.g. vinegar, orange juice, chocolate, ginger, garlic, pencil shavings) and see if the children can guess what they are.

5. The children can use mirrors to look closely at the taste buds on their tongue. They could also use mirrors to look at what happens to the pupils of their eyes when they go into a darker room or outside in the sunshine. The pupils will dilate — get bigger — when they are in a darker place, to enable more light to enter the eye, and the opposite should happen when they go into a brighter area. (Ensure that pupils do not look directly into the Sun or other light source.)

Year 1: Section Three — Animals

Mammals

> **Learning Objectives:**
> - To recognise common features of mammals.
> - To know that humans are mammals.
> - To understand that mammals live in different habitats.
> - To read and spell scientific vocabulary relating to animals.
>
> **Year 1 Science Programme of Study**
> "Identify and name a variety of common animals including mammals. Describe and compare the structure of a variety of common animals."

Preparation: Provide sticky notes and felt pens — enough for each member of the class, and a large sheet of paper with the word 'mammals' in the middle.

Have some picture story books or non-fiction books about different types of animals available for the children to look at.

Prepare cards for the 'Make a Mammal' activity (see opposite page).

Lesson Activities

1. Ask each child to write the name of an animal on a sticky note. Then, either in groups or as a whole class, ask them to think of how they could put these animals into groups. For example, they may decide to group them according to size, diet, number of legs, etc.

2. Explain that scientists classify animals by putting them into groups (called 'classes') of animals that have certain features in common. Humans belong in the class called mammals — we will be learning about these today.

3. Read page 24 of the Activity Book together.

4. Talk through each feature and use these to reinforce the fact that humans are mammals, as we satisfy all of these criteria.

5. Look again at the animals that the children wrote on their sticky notes. Which of these are mammals? Stick them onto a large sheet of paper around the word 'mammals'. (Keep the remaining animal sticky notes for the next few lessons.)

6. Discuss the different places where mammals live around the world. Address any queries or misconceptions that arise about mammals. For example, children may not realise that mammals which live in water (e.g. whales or dolphins) breathe with lungs, so they need to come to the surface for air. You can explain that fish — which they will learn more about in a later lesson — have gills rather than lungs, which means that they can breathe in water.

Extension Ideas

*If you feel that it is appropriate at this stage, briefly introduce the other classes of animals: **birds** (with feathers), **fish** (with fins and scales), **reptiles** (which have scaly skin) and **amphibians** (these are born in the water but the adults live on land) — they will learn more about these in the next few lessons.*

*You could also explain that all of the animals are **vertebrates**, which means that they have a backbone; as opposed to **invertebrates**, which do not have a backbone (e.g. insects, spiders and crabs).*

Extension Ideas
"Did you know...?"
- *Whales and dolphins do have hair, but only when they are fetuses or very young.*
- *Two Australian mammals — platypuses and echidnas — lay eggs rather than giving birth to live young.*

7. Ask pupils to work through page 25 of the Activity Book. Address any misconceptions and refer back to the features on the previous page.

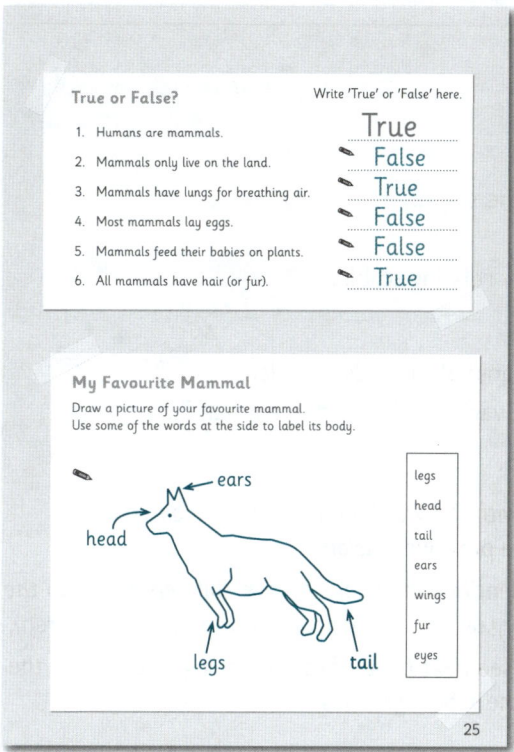

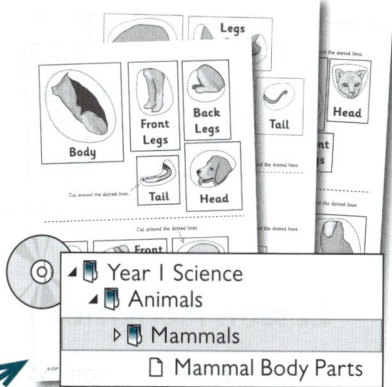

Extension Ideas
Introduce other body parts, such as whiskers or claws, for the children to add to their labelled pictures.

8. When they are drawing their favourite mammal, it may help to have some animal names and pictures to prompt them (e.g. providing books for them to look at). You should also point out that they may not need to use all of the labels for the body parts.

9. Hand out the cards showing body parts of different mammals and ask the children to read the labels on the cards. They should cut out the body parts and can either put them together to make the correct mammals, or mix them up with other members of the class to make new mammals.

Extension Ideas
*Ask the children to make up names for their new mammals, using parts of the different animals' names, e.g. a c-rab-d-at (**c**at's head, **rab**bit's ears, **d**og's body, **rat**'s tail).*

Plenary Questions

1. What type of animals have we been learning about today?
2. What features do they have in common?
3. Where do mammals live?
4. Do any of the children have pets at home that are mammals? What makes these animals good pets?

Follow-Up Ideas

1. Ask the questions: "What mammals do you think there are in our local area?" and "What evidence can we find of them?". Take the children outside into the school grounds or local park so that they can use their senses to find signs of mammals. For example, they may see a hole in the soil where a badger has been looking for worms or a squirrel has buried a nut; they could spot a mound of earth that shows where a mole has popped up, or a hole where a family of foxes has made their den; they could find trees that have had bark stripped off by squirrels; they may even find mammal footprints in wet mud and could make plaster casts of these to take back to the classroom.

2. Ask the children to draw, paint or make models of different mammals for a class display. They can write their own labels or facts.

3. If children have pets at home, ask them to keep a diary for a week (using words, drawings or photos) of what their pets do, eat, etc.

Birds

> **Learning Objectives:**
> - To recognise the features of birds.
> - To understand that not all birds are the same.
> - To identify some common birds.
> - To read and spell scientific vocabulary relating to birds.
>
> **Year 1 Science Programme of Study**
> "Identify and name a variety of common animals including birds.
> Describe and compare the structure of a variety of common animals."

Preparation: Provide a large sheet of paper with the word 'birds' in the middle, and the animal sticky notes from the previous session.

If possible, provide some bird identification books or give children access to the RSPB Kids website (www.rspb.org.uk/discoverandenjoynature/families/children).

Prepare the bird picture sheet (see next page) if you are going to carry out the suggested follow-up activity in the school grounds.

Lesson Activities

1. Write the question "What is a bird?" and ask the children to talk about this to a partner. Take feedback from the pairs and record their ideas.

2. Look back at the animals the children wrote on sticky notes in the previous session. Are any of these birds?
   If so, stick them onto a large sheet of paper around the word 'birds'.

3. Read the first part of page 26 in the Activity Book together.

4. Discuss each feature of birds and add any new information to the ideas the children gave earlier.

5. Talk about how birds are similar to humans (e.g. we have eyes, legs) and different from humans (e.g. birds lay eggs rather than give birth to live babies, birds have feathers while we have hair to keep us warm).

6. Highlight the use of the words 'all' and 'many' ("**All** birds have wings and **many** can fly"), to show that not all birds are exactly the same.

7. Look at the pictures of common birds at the bottom of page 26 of the Activity Book. You may want to point out that gulls are more commonly referred to as 'seagulls', but that they don't all live by the sea, so 'gull' is the correct term.

Phonics & Spelling Links

Use the words 'bird' and 'blackbird' (plus 'birch' and 'fir' from the Plants section) when teaching the 'ir' sound.

Extension Ideas

Feathers are not just for warmth. Discuss other reasons why birds have feathers. (They help birds to fly, they're waterproof, they can be used as camouflage and they help some birds float on water.)

Extension Question

Can any of the children name a bird that does not fly (e.g. ostrich, emu) or can't fly very far (e.g. chicken, peacock)?

8. Ask the children to describe the birds shown in the pictures (e.g. colours, shapes of beaks, lengths of tails) and tell you which (if any) of these birds they have seen in their garden, the school grounds or their local area. Invite children to come and add more bird names to your 'birds' sheet.

9. Ask pupils to work through page 27 of the Activity Book. You may need to explain how to complete the crossword.

Extension Ideas

- *Ask children to choose one of the birds from the pictures and to write a sentence to describe it, using the vocabulary they have learnt.*

- *Can anyone describe or name any other birds they have seen? Use a bird identification book or the RSPB website (go to www.rspb.org.uk and enter 'Bird Identifier' into the search box) to identify any unknown birds.*

Plenary Questions

1. How are baby birds born?
2. Which body parts do birds have?
3. How are birds different from humans?
4. Which birds have you seen in your garden / on the playground / in the park? Does anyone (or a family member) have a pet bird at home?

Follow-Up Ideas

1. Print out the birds picture sheet and use this to help the children identify birds in the school grounds. They can either tick off the bird species they see or record numbers of each bird using a tally. Ideally, the children should watch the birds from a window and you may decide to put some food out (on a bird table or just on the playground) to attract more birds. N.B. Female sparrows, blackbirds and chaffinches look different to males, and there are different types of gulls, pigeons and sparrows, but the pictures given should be sufficient for this age group.

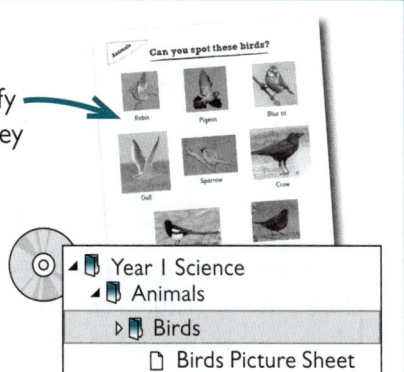

2. The picture sheets could also be used for a 'Guess the Bird' game, where the children either give clues to a partner (e.g. "I have an orange beak") or their partner asks questions (e.g. "Do you have a blue head?") to guess which bird they are thinking of.

3. Let the children explore the information and activities on the RSPB Early Birds website: www.rspb.org.uk/discoverandenjoynature/families/children/earlyyears/index.aspx

4. Make some plastic bottle bird feeders or bird cakes to feed the birds in your school grounds, or for the children to take home to put in their gardens. The RSPB Early Birds website also has information on other bird/nature activities which you could try.

Year 1: Section Three — Animals

Fish

> **Learning Objectives:**
> - To know how fish are different from other animals.
> - To name some species of fish.
> - To group and classify using observations from secondary sources.
> - To read and spell scientific vocabulary relating to animals that live in water.
>
> **Year 1 Science Programme of Study**
> "Identify and name a variety of common animals including fish.
> Describe and compare the structure of a variety of common animals."

Preparation: If possible, bring in a whole fish bought from the supermarket.
Prepare cards for the activities described on the opposite page.
Provide a large sheet of paper with the word 'fish' in the middle,
and the animal sticky notes from previous sessions.

Lesson Activities

1. Ask the children to name as many animals as they can, stating where each animal lives. Encourage a wide range of species including pets. Expect such answers as **lion** (Africa, zoo); **dog** (house); **bird** (cage, tree). Ask the children to name some animals that live in water.

2. As a class, look at the photos of aquatic animals on page 28 of the Activity Book.

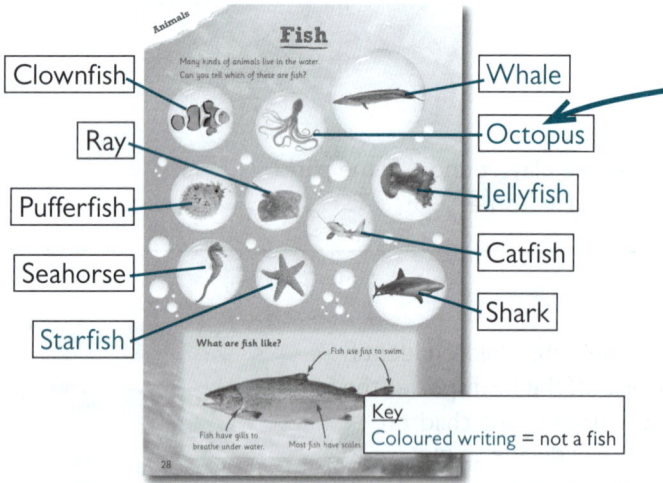

3. Can they name any of them? Encourage the children to look closely at the pictures and to suggest two of the pictures which have something in common (other than living in water) and discuss their ideas.

4. Recap that scientists group animals by what they have in common — one of these groups of animals is "Fish". Explain that not all creatures that live in water are fish and that to be included in the group they must have certain structures. Use the Activity Book to share the structures common to fish.

5. Look back at the animals the children wrote on sticky notes in the earlier session. Are any of these fish? If so, stick them onto a large sheet of paper around the word 'fish' and invite children to write the names of other fish they now know.

Extension Ideas

Introduce the pupils to the idea that there are different types of aquatic environments such as saltwater (seas and oceans), freshwater (rivers and ponds) and man-made (fish tanks and aquariums) and that the animals found in each of these are usually suited to that environment.

Teacher Notes

It is intended that the photographs in the Activity Book be used as a focus for class discussion through observation and questioning. It is not expected that the children will recognise or be able to name all of the creatures. Pupils should be encouraged to observe differences and to understand that although fish may look different from each other, there are fixed structures that are always there if they are to be classified as fish.

Extension Activity

Ask the children to select two of the creatures that appear to have very little in common and to explain their choices.

Gills extract oxygen from the water.

The overlapping structure of **scales** provides protection but still allows fish to bend their bodies. Scales also let fish glide smoothly through the water. Scales of many fish are made from dentine (or a similar substance called cosmin) which is the same material that teeth are made from.

Fins are used instead of legs to help the fish move. The fin around the tail tends to be the main propulsive organ. Fins on the back tend to be for balance, and fins around the shoulder or hip girdles are used for steering.

34 Year 1: Section Three — Animals

6. If you have been able to bring in a whole fish, investigate the features of the fish as a class. For example, investigate the structure of scales by asking a pupil to stroke them one way then the other and explain to the rest of the class how it feels. Make sure they wash their hands afterwards though!

7. Ask pupils to work through page 29 of the Activity Book.

Phonics & Spelling Links

Use the words 'fish' and 'shark' when teaching the 'sh' sound.

Extension Activity

Ask the more able to label the fins, scales and gills on their drawing.

Early finishers could make a selection of water animals from modelling materials or to write a "sentence" about their favourite water animal.

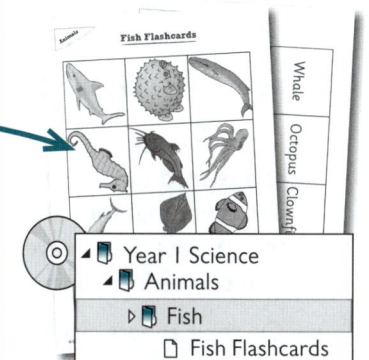

8. Use the cards prepared from the Fish Flashcards sheet provided.
   a. Use two copies of each picture and place all the cards face down. The children should take turns to choose a pair of cards to reveal. If a matching pair of pictures is revealed then the child keeps that pair. When all the cards have been matched, the game ends.
   b. Use one copy of each picture and its corresponding name card. Place all the cards face down. The children can take turns to choose a pair of cards to reveal. If the picture and the name of the creature match, then the child keeps that pair. When all the cards have been matched, the game ends.
   c. Finally, ask the children to sort the water animals into two piles — "Fish" and "Not Fish". Ask pupils to explain their choices. Discuss how the names of creatures can be misleading — jellyfish and starfish do not have gills and fins, so they aren't actually fish!

Plenary Questions

1. What have we learned today about animals that live in water?
2. What structures do fish have to help them live underwater?
3. Do any of the children keep fish at home? Are all kinds of fish suitable for keeping as pets? Why not?

Follow-Up Ideas

1. Ask children to bring in pictures of water animals for a class display. Ask them to write labels for their pictures or facts they have found out about them.
2. Ask the children for as many words as possible to describe fish. Use these to write poems.
3. Provide the children with different sizes of fish cut from card. Ask them to compare and order the fish by size. Ask questions such as "Which one is the longest?" and "Which of these two is thinner?". Where appropriate this could be extended to measuring the fish.

Year 1: Section Three — Animals   35

What do Animals Eat?

> **Learning Objectives:**
> - To understand that animals eat different things, and this is called their 'diet'.
> - To know what the terms 'carnivore', 'herbivore' and 'omnivore' mean.
> - To identify some examples of carnivores, herbivores and omnivores.
>
> **Year 1 Science Programme of Study**
> "Identify and name a variety of common animals that are carnivores, herbivores and omnivores."

Preparation: Provide a large sheet of paper and selection of coloured pens per group/table.

Provide each child (or pair) with a small mirror.

Prepare the 'We're Going on a Bug Hunt!' sheet (see over) and provide materials for invertebrate collection (pots, hand lenses, spoons/paintbrushes/pooters) if you are going to carry out the suggested follow-up activity in the school grounds.

Lesson Activities

1. In groups, ask the children to discuss their favourite foods and record them on their sheets of paper.
   Tell them that they are going to identify food that comes from plants (fruit, leaves, seeds, vegetables, etc.) and food that comes from animals (meat, eggs, dairy products).

2. On their sheets, ask the children to circle examples of the two different types of food in different colours.
   You may need to help them with foods that are less obvious. For example, bread and pasta originate from wheat, which is a plant.

3. Record some of their ideas on a flip chart under the headings 'plants' and 'meat'. Explain that humans are able to eat both meat and plants (although some people choose not to eat certain foods, due to religious, moral or health reasons) and this makes us 'omnivores'.

4. They can use mirrors to look at their teeth, identifying the ones that they use for eating different types of food (e.g. flat ones at the back for grinding up food such as vegetables, sharp ones at the front for cutting foods such as meat).

5. Read page 30 of the Activity Book together.

6. Discuss the example animals given on the page. Can the children think of any others for each category (e.g. lions as carnivores, tortoises as herbivores, humans as omnivores)? You could also ask them to identify which of the animals on the sheet are mammals, birds or fish, to recap learning from previous lessons.

Extension Ideas
You could introduce the names of the different types of teeth (molars at the back, incisors at the front and canines at the side).

Teacher Notes
Help children to read the words 'carnivore', 'herbivore' and 'omnivore' by breaking down the first part of the word and then adding 'vore' (this comes from a Latin word meaning 'to devour').

*CAR - NI - VORE, HER - BI - VORE,
OM - NI - VORE*

Can they think of any ways of remembering the meanings of the different words? For example, herbs are a type of plant (although you may then need to point out that this doesn't mean that herbivores only eat herbs). Omnivores say "om-nom-nom" as they eat everything!

Teacher Notes
Pupils may be interested to know that, while most land snails are herbivores, aquatic snails (snails that live in water) are usually omnivores.

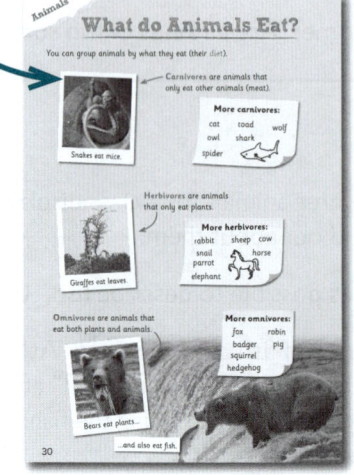

Year 1: Section Three — Animals

7. Ask the children to work through page 31 of the Activity Book:

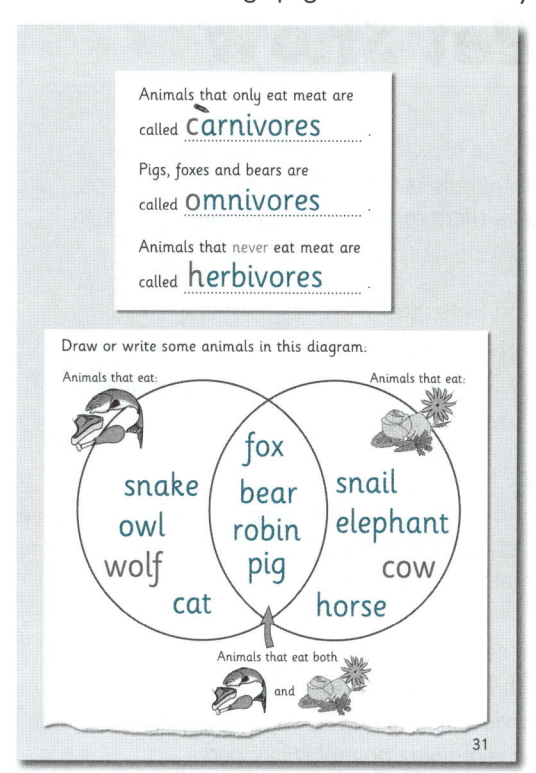

Phonics & Spelling Links

Use the word 'eat' to reinforce the spelling of 'meat'. E.g. "You eat meat (but you meet and greet.)"

Extension Ideas

Look at pictures (search online) or models/skulls (a local nature centre or secondary school may have some of these) showing the teeth of carnivores, herbivores and omnivores.

Discuss the functions of the different types of teeth and compare them to the children's own teeth. For example, carnivores tend to have much larger canine teeth, herbivores have wider molars and omnivores' teeth are more similar to ours.

Explain how the diagram on page 31 works and how to fill it in. Introduce the term 'Venn diagram' if you wish. Encourage the children to include animals from the previous page and to add in any more they can think of. They can choose whether to draw, write or both, and each child should aim to include at least ten animals in total.

Extension Activity

Early finishers can write sentences explaining what carnivores, herbivores and omnivores are, including examples.

8. You could point out that the word 'a' is used before 'carnivore' and 'herbivore' (because they both start with a consonant), but 'an' is used before 'omnivore' (because it starts with a vowel).

Plenary Questions

1. What is a carnivore? Can you give an example of an animal that only eats meat?
2. What is a herbivore? Can you give an example of an animal that only eats plants?
3. What is an omnivore? Can you give an example of an animal that eats meat and plants?

Follow-Up Ideas

1. Print out copies of the sheet 'We're Going on a Bug Hunt!' and take the children into the school grounds to look for examples of carnivores, herbivores and omnivores. If possible, take out equipment for the children to collect and study the invertebrates ('minibeasts') that they find.
   They could also draw their favourites. Ensure that you talk to the children about how to handle the animals (i.e. "kind hands", use a paintbrush/spoon/pooter to collect them gently), and that they understand to put them back where they found them.

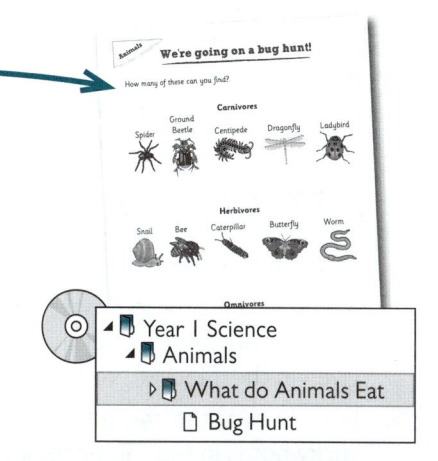

2. Use PE hoops and toy animals (or laminated pictures) to make large scale Venn diagrams. The children can write labels for the different sections. These could be photographed for display or used as an interactive classroom display.

3. The children could use books or the Internet to research common animals and create fact files about their diets: "I am a…", "I eat…", "this means I am a…", "here is a picture of me…".

Year 1: Section Three — Animals

At the Pet Show

*'At the Pet Show' is a **synoptic topic** for the Animals section. It builds on the concepts introduced in the preceding sessions and applies them to a real-world context.*

Learning Objectives:
- To identify some animals that make good pets, and why.
- To recognise that not all animals make good pets, and the reasons for this.
- To understand that pet owners have a responsibility to look after their animals properly, as they rely on their owners for all of their needs.

Year 1 Science Programme of Study
"Identify and name a variety of common animals including fish, amphibians, reptiles, birds and mammals. Describe and compare the structure of a variety of common animals (fish, amphibians, reptiles, birds and mammals, including pets)."

Preparation: Provide a large sheet of paper with the word 'reptile' on the left and 'amphibian' on the right. Also provide the 'mammal', 'bird' and 'fish' sheets from the previous lessons and any remaining animal sticky notes.

You may want to prepare some information cards about animals that make, or do not make, good pets (see Lesson Activity points 2 and 3 below).

Lesson Activities

1. Ask all the children who have a pet (or whose family members have one) to stand up, but not to reveal what animals their pets are. Invite some of the children to do impressions of their pets for everyone else to guess, encouraging them to act out the animals' body parts (ears, tail, four legs, etc.).

2. Discuss some of the reasons why these animals make good pets, for example they might be furry to stroke, easy to look after, loyal, funny, interesting/unusual, provide security, friendship, comfort, etc.

3. Now ask some different children to stand up and do impressions of animals that do not make good pets, for example a fierce animal like a lion, a large animal such as an elephant, or a wild animal such as a badger. (It may be a good idea to have some prompt cards in case the children can't think of any animals.)

4. Recap the classes of animals that they have already looked at — these are mammals, birds and fish. (See the Teacher Notes on the right for a recap.)

5. Introduce two more classes of animals — reptiles and amphibians. Further information on these is given in the Teacher Notes on the right.

6. Look back at the animals the children wrote on sticky notes in the earlier session. Are any of these reptiles or amphibians? If so, stick them onto a large sheet of paper around the correct word.

7. Read pages 32-33 of the Activity Book together.

Teacher Notes

Mammals
Most mammals give birth to live young, which they feed on milk. They have a backbone (spine), have hair/fur, and use lungs to breathe air.

Birds
Birds lay eggs and breathe with lungs. They have feathers to keep them warm, beaks for eating, claws on their feet, a backbone, a tail, and wings (which many use for flying).

Fish
Fish have fins for swimming and most have scales on their skin. They have a backbone, and they breathe under water using gills.

Reptiles
Reptiles lay eggs and breathe with lungs. They have scaly skin and a backbone. Examples include: snakes, lizards, crocodiles, alligators, turtles, tortoises.

Amphibians
Amphibians breathe with lungs. They have a backbone, and soft skin that must be kept moist. They lay their eggs in water, where their young live, but the adults then live on land. Examples include: frogs, toads, newts, salamanders.

Year 1: Section Three — Animals

8. Read the information about each animal and ask the children to describe the animals' body parts from the pictures. Invite children to add these animals to the large sheets of paper with the classes (mammals, birds, fish, reptiles and amphibians) written on them.

9. Ask the children if they can remember what 'carnivores', 'herbivores' and 'omnivores' are, and group the animals from the Activity Book pages into the correct categories. (Crocodile, tree frog, tiger, newt and owl are carnivores; rabbit, budgie and tortoise are herbivores; goldfish is an omnivore.)

10. Discuss whether or not each of the animals on the sheet would make a good pet, giving reasons. Talk about why it is important to give pet animals the correct diet and to meet all their other requirements, as pet owners have a responsibility to look after their pets.

11. Ask pupils to complete the activities in the Activity Book, using the information given.

Phonics & Spelling Links

Use the words 'reptile' and 'crocodile' to check pupils' understanding of the split digraph 'i–e'.

Extension Activity

Early finishers can write a speech bubble for someone who would want one of the other animals as a pet. For example, "I want a bird that's an herbivore" for the budgie.

Plenary Questions

1. Can you give me an example of a mammal/bird/fish/reptile/amphibian?
2. Which animals make good pets, and why?
3. Which animals would not make good pets, and why?
4. What do carnivores/herbivores/omnivores eat?
5. Why do pet owners have a responsibility to look after their pets properly?

Follow-Up Ideas

1. Ask the children to make their own pet show. They should design information cards for different animals of their choice, similar to those in the Activity Book. You can find templates for the information cards on the CD-ROM.

2. Prepare a set of A3 sheets, each with one of the following words written on it: mammal, fish, bird, reptile, amphibian. Set up 5 stations around the classroom, each labelled with the name of a different class of animal. Then show a slideshow of different animals on the IWB, e.g.: rickcollinsphotographyonline.com/galleries/wildlife-2/slideshow-2/ For each animal shown, ask the children to stand by the correct sign.

3. Ask the children to make posters or leaflets showing pet owners how to look after their animals. They should include information on correct diet, shelter, warmth, play, exercise, etc.

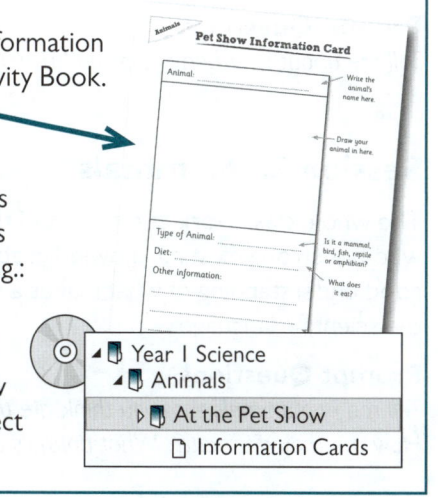

Year 1: Section Three — Animals

Notes on Assessment (Animals)

You'll need to assess pupils' understanding of both the knowledge-based requirements from the Science Programme of Study and the 'Working Scientifically' requirements that underpin the Key Stage 1 curriculum.

The 'Animals' section gives opportunities for pupils to **work scientifically** by:
- Observing closely, using simple equipment.
- Identifying and classifying animals.
- Using their observations and ideas to suggest answers to questions.

The tasks pupils complete in the **Activity Book** will help you assess pupils' understanding of the 'Animals, including humans' section of the Year 1 Programme of Study.

For both the 'Animals, including humans' section of the Programme of Study and the 'Working Scientifically' requirements, you can use **Classroom Assessment**.

This will allow pupils who may not have strong literacy skills to demonstrate their understanding practically and verbally.

Year 1 Science Programme of Study: ANIMALS, INCLUDING HUMANS	KS1 Science: Working Scientifically
Identify and name a variety of common animals including fish, amphibians, reptiles, birds and mammals / Identify and name a variety of common animals that are carnivores, herbivores and omnivores / Describe and compare the structure of a variety of common animals (fish, amphibians, reptiles, birds and mammals, including pets) / Identify, name, draw and label the basic parts of the human body and say which part of the body is associated with each sense	Observing closely, using simple equipment / Identifying and classifying animals / Using their observations and ideas to suggest answers to questions

Classroom Assessment

Classroom Assessment should be in the form of small-group work, observation and the use of open-ended questions. Try focusing on just five or six pupils in each lesson, so you get a deeper understanding of the level they're working at.

Session 1: The Human Body

Choose one group to observe as they draw around a body and label it. Notice who is able to name all of the different body parts without support and who has a good understanding of their functions and associated senses. At this age some children may have much more advanced knowledge about the human body — make notes about this on your assessment sheet and use the extension questions and activities to move their learning on.

Prompt Questions
Tell me about your body. Do you know any other parts? What does this part do?

Y1 Science PoS: Animals, inc. humans				Working Scientifically		
			✓			✓

Session 2: Mammals

The whole class work at the start of this lesson is a good opportunity to find out who has strong existing knowledge about animal life. Note who demonstrates a good understanding of what makes a mammal and who needs support to understand the scientific language.

Prompt Questions
Tell me two animals that you think are the same in some way. Explain your answer. How are they different? What animals are humans most like?

Y1 Science PoS: Animals, inc. humans				Working Scientifically	
✓	✓			✓	✓

Session 3: Birds

Use this lesson to focus on your less able scientists. Go back over the classifications of animals and see if they can name one animal from each group. Support pupils as they work in the Activity Book and ask them to describe the birds on the page, encouraging the use of vocabulary (such as 'wings', 'feathers', 'beak', 'egg', 'fly'), and note their descriptions down.

Prompt Questions
Can you name one of these birds? Tell me about it. What do you know about birds? How do they travel? Where do baby birds come from?

Session 4: Fish

Choose a small group or several mixed ability pairs that you will work with while the class is completing the independent work. Use the Fish Flashcards and play one or two of the games suggested on page 35 of this Teacher Book. Which children demonstrate a good understanding of which water animals are fish and which are not? Encourage children to compare the animals and say whether or not they think each animal is a fish, and why.

Intervention
Make sure all of the children you work with are clear about the difference between fish and other water animals, using appropriate language to describe the differences.

Session 5: What do Animals Eat?

You are now moving on to a different way of classifying animals — using their diet. Use the plenary questions of this lesson to give pupils the opportunity to talk in pairs about the questions. Select a few pairs to listen to and notice who has grasped the difference between carnivores, herbivores and omnivores and which pupils can give several examples, both from the lesson and their existing knowledge of animals.

Session 6: At the Pet Show

This lesson will be a good chance to pick out any children who you haven't yet observed or talked to over the course of the topic. While children are working independently you could call pupils up one at a time to assess them against the learning objectives. Which children are now familiar with how to classify animals? Who is able to identify and describe a range of animals from each category? Who needs support to remember the differences between each class of animal?

Prompt Questions
What is your favourite animal? Tell me about it. I wonder if you know what type of animal it is. Can you explain how you know this? What features does it have that makes it a mammal/bird/etc.?

Recording Pupils' Attainment

By the end of the topic, you should be confident in your judgement of which pupils in your class have met the topic's learning objectives. You should also know which pupils are yet to meet the learning objectives and which children have moved beyond the Year One Programme of Study with additional skills and knowledge.

Record pupils' attainment in the Assessment Grid on the CD-ROM. You may wish to use a traffic light system to colour-code the grid.

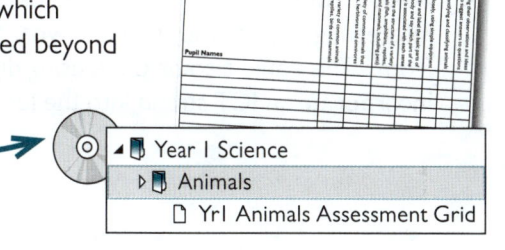

Year 1: Section Four — Materials
What's it Made From?

Learning Objectives:
- To learn the names of some common materials and their features.
- To be able to say what material an object is made from.

Year 1 Science Programme of Study
"Distinguish between an object and the material from which it is made. Identify and name a variety of everyday materials, including wood, plastic, glass, metal, water and rock."

Preparation: Put together a selection of objects made from different materials. Sort them into 'odd one out' sets (two objects of one material and one of a different material, e.g. two wooden objects and one made of metal).

Lesson Activities

1. Show the class three objects, e.g. a wooden spoon, a wooden toy train and a metal saucepan.

2. Ask pupils to discuss in pairs which object is the odd one out and why. They can then explain their reasons to the rest of the class.

3. Draw out any references to the materials the objects are made from and note the two materials (wood and metal) on the white board.

4. Reinforce the difference between the name of the object and the material it is made from.

5. Read the top half of pages 34-35 of the Activity Book together:

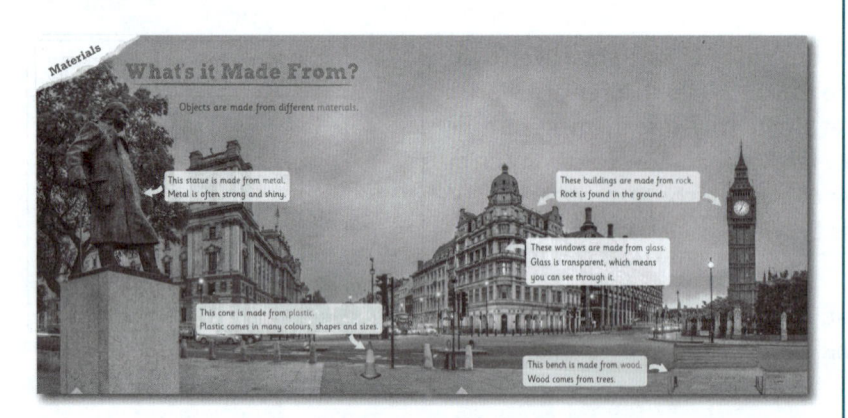

6. Go on a 'materials treasure hunt'. This could either be done independently or in pairs around the classroom, or you could take the whole class around the school grounds.

7. Ask the pupils to record using words and pictures any interesting objects they find and what material they are made from. This could also be done using digital cameras to incorporate an ICT strand into the lesson.

Extension Idea

Your discussion may also include some of the properties of different materials.

For example, some children might note that the saucepan is shiny, while the spoon and the train are not. Why is this?

You could include two different metal objects in one set that have different properties, so that one is bendy and one is not. Note the words and save them for the next lesson.

Hard or soft?
What happens when you knock on or scratch a material?

Stretchy or stiff?
Can the material be easily stretched and does it return to its original shape?

Shiny or dull?
What happens when you shine a torch on the object?

Rough or smooth?
Run your fingers across the surface of the objects. What do the materials feel like?

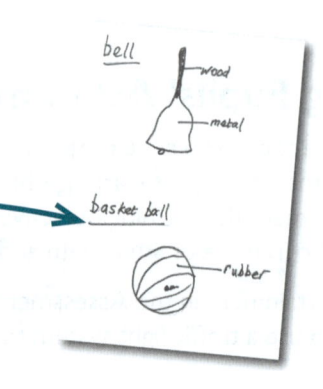

42 Year 1: Section Four — Materials

8. Ask pupils to work through the activities on pages 34-35 of the Activity Book:

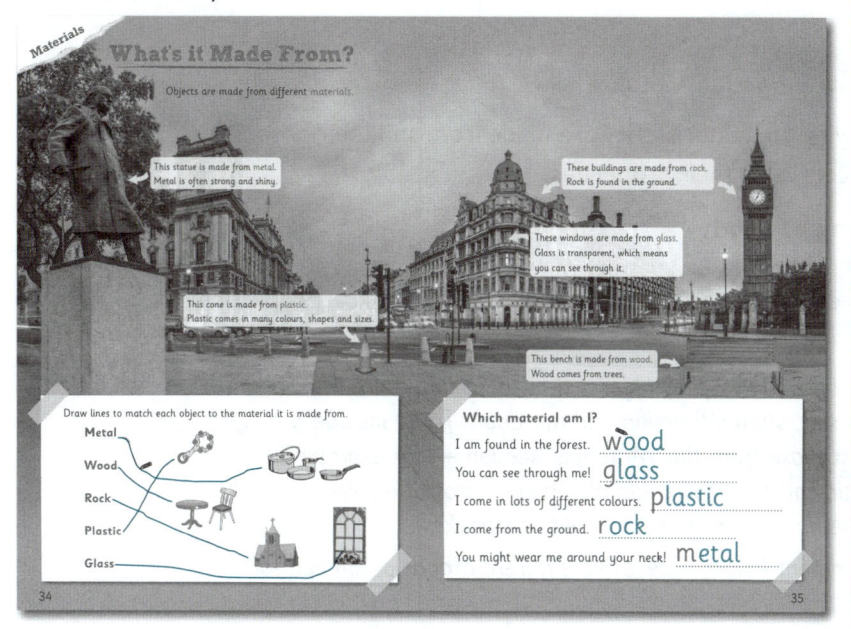

Extension Ideas

- Show the class a glass of water. Can water be used as a material to make objects from?
- Discuss snowmen, ice sculptures and igloos. You might like to show images of these from the Internet on the IWB.
- What has to happen to water before it can be made into an object?
- What are the drawbacks of making things out of water or ice?

Extension Questions

Ask early finishers to think about why each material was chosen to make each object.

- Why make a chair from wood instead of glass?
- Why make a saucepan from metal instead of plastic?

Plenary Questions

1. What materials have we learned about today?
   Can anyone remember all five?

2. Can anyone spot anything in the room that is made from two different materials?
   Three? Four?

3. How can we tell what material something is made from?
   What are some good clues to look for?

Follow-Up Ideas

1. Ask pupils to complete the 'Materials at Home' worksheet on the CD-ROM. They could take a photo or draw a picture of their home and think about what materials have been used to make it. They should label which parts of the house have been made from which material and start to think about why each material has been chosen to do a particular job.

2. Investigate as a class the homes of other people from around the world. What materials are these homes made from?

3. Tell the story of the three little pigs. Link back to the children's knowledge of materials and discuss what each house is made from (straw, sticks and bricks). Pupils could work in groups to try to build a house for a toy pig from a selection of materials such as straw, cardboard, plastic bottles, toy bricks, etc. Which material works best? Why?

4. Ask pupils to think about when they go swimming (or bring in a swimming kit to show the class — including swim suit, hat, goggles, towel and some pool toys). What materials have been used to make each item? Why have they been chosen? Pupils could then investigate materials that are waterproof. Tell pupils that years ago, when people went swimming they might have worn a knitted swimsuit made from wool! Is wool a good material to make a swim suit out of? Why or why not?

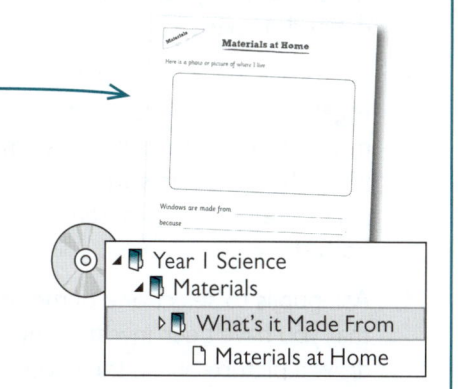

Talking About Materials

Learning Objectives:
- To describe objects by saying the material they are made from and their properties.
- To sort and compare objects using their properties.

Year 1 Science Programme of Study
"Describe the simple physical properties of a variety of everyday materials. Compare and group together a variety of everyday materials on the basis of their physical properties."

Preparation: Collect between 10 and 20 everyday objects that the children are familiar with. They should vary in size, shape, function and material. Try to include a range of materials, not just those from the 'Materials' session — for example brick, paper, fabrics, elastic and foil. You could also take photos of a selection of the objects and print them ready to stick into children's books.

For the Quick Experiment below, collect five different brands of kitchen roll.

Lesson Activities

1. Sit the class in a circle and in the middle place your selection of everyday objects. Let pupils spend some time investigating and exploring the objects. Ask the children to talk in pairs and choose two objects that are similar in some way and then explain their reasoning to the class. Some children might reference materials from the previous session.

2. Discuss some of the properties of different materials — this may be a recap if you covered this in the previous session. List some key words for pupils to use when describing materials: hard/soft, stretchy/stiff, shiny/dull, rough/smooth. (These were introduced and defined on page 42.)

3. Read page 36 of the Activity Book together. Ask children to repeat the pairing task (point 1), but this time they must choose objects with similar properties — e.g. two items that are both shiny.

4. Ask pupils to select one of the objects that you have been investigating and draw a picture of it in their science book (alternatively you can have digital photos printed and ready to stick in). Then ask the children to complete the following sentences to describe the object:

   This is a .... It is made from .... and it is .... and ....

Remind children to choose 'properties' words for their descriptions. Children may complete descriptions of up to three or four different objects.

Extension Ideas

- Other properties may also come up in discussion such as: waterproof/not waterproof, will float/won't float and absorbent/not absorbent. Explore what these words mean and come up with examples of everyday objects that need to have these properties.
- Brainstorm some objects which are transparent and opaque. Ask pupils whether they can think of any objects which they can almost see through, but not quite (e.g. stained glass, frosted glass, some milk cartons). Introduce the word 'translucent' — the light can travel through but you can't see objects clearly through them.
- "I get caught in the rain when walking home with my shopping. In my bag I have a jumper, a magazine and some tin foil. Which should I use to cover my head? Why? Can you think of any other everyday items that might make a good umbrella?"

Quick Experiment

Which brand of kitchen roll is the most absorbent? Collect five different brands of kitchen roll (from value to well known). Ask the children to predict which is best at mopping up spills.

Place a piece of each kitchen roll into coloured water for 20 seconds then ring out the contents into a measuring beaker. Which absorbed the most? Were their predictions correct?

5. Ask pupils to work through page 37 of the Activity Book:

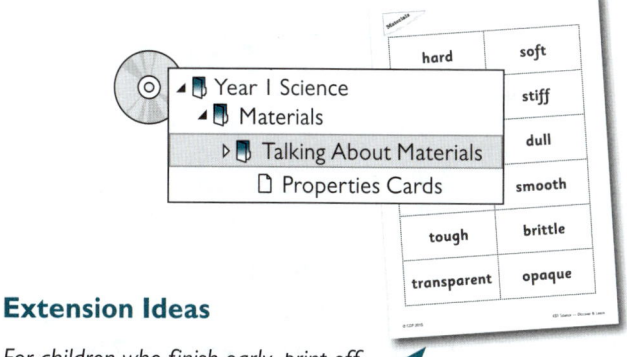

Odd one out!
Put a circle around the object you think is the odd one out. Remember to think about the properties of each object.

bell   spoon   ring
The bell and the ring are **shiny** but the spoon is **dull**.

ruler   plank of wood   metal beam
The plank of wood and the metal beam are **tough** but the ruler is **brittle**.

cup   mug   glass
The **cup** and the **glass** are **transparent** but the **mug** is **opaque**.

spring   rubber band   pencil
The spring and the rubber band are flexible, but pencil is stiff.

37

Extension Ideas

For children who finish early, print off cards with different properties on.

Children could sort these into pairs of opposites (e.g. rough and smooth). They could play a memory game with a partner: with the cards face up, one pupil closes their eyes and the other pupil takes one of the cards away. The first pupil then tries to work out which one is missing.

Alternatively, with the cards face down, one pupil could pick a card and then describe the property on their card (without using the actual word) for the other pupil to guess. This could also be played as a class activity.

Plenary Questions

1. Which 'properties' words have we learned today? Talk in pairs and see how many you can remember.

2. How is a toothbrush handle different from the bristles? Use properties words to explain.

3. Tell me two things in our classroom that are similar in some way. How are they also different?

Follow-Up Ideas

1. Ask pupils to look at any drinks containers they come across at home or while out and about (glass tumbler, juice cartons, polystyrene coffee cup, plastic bottles, etc.) and use their findings to complete the worksheet on the CD-ROM. What material has been used to make each container? Why? What properties does that material have? You could ask children to report their findings back and discuss the materials according to whether they are meant to last, are disposable or can be recycled. Here is a nice infographic that shows the impact of disposable coffee cups: www.mnn.com/lifestyle/responsible-living/blogs/infographic-why-reuse-a-cup
Discuss with children the benefits to the environment of taking reusable drinks containers when they go out, instead of disposable ones.

2. Investigate which materials can be recycled. This website is a good resource to use: www.recyclezone.org.uk
Make sure you have a visible class recycling bin and/or compost bin, and ask children to design posters to show which materials can be put in each.

3. In an art lesson, pupils could make stained glass windows using black sugar paper and coloured tracing paper. Display these on the classroom windows along with the words *translucent*, *transparent* and *opaque*. Discuss what these words mean in relation to the properties of different materials.

In the Allotment

*'In the Allotment' is a **synoptic topic** for the Materials section. It builds on the concepts introduced in the preceding sessions and applies them to a real-world context.*

Learning Objectives:
- To learn the names of some common materials and their features.
- To be able to say what an object is made from.
- To describe objects by saying the material they are made from and their properties.

Year 1 Science Programme of Study
"Identify and name a variety of materials, including wood, plastic, glass, metal, water and rock. Describe the simple physical properties of a variety of everyday materials."

Preparation: Arrange a class outing to a local garden — a school garden, local allotment or public garden would work well. Pupils will be designing and making their own Materials Garden, so they will need a selection of resources to work with, e.g. collage materials, old gardening magazines, junk items, paper and art supplies.

Garden Visit

Take the class to a local garden or allotment.

Ask pupils to spot as many different materials in the environment as they can and discuss what each one is called, why it has been chosen and some of its important properties.

Example: "A greenhouse is made out of glass, which is transparent, brittle and waterproof. It has been chosen to create a warm environment for plants to grow."

If you are not able to visit a garden, use the slide show on the CD-ROM of different outdoor spaces, which feature a range of materials.

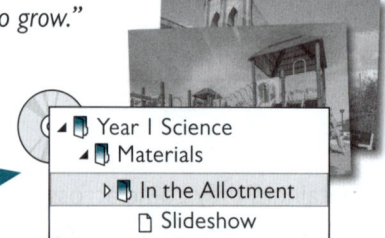

Classroom Activities

1. Ask pupils to work through pages 38-39 of the Activity Book, labelling what each item is made from, and one of the key properties of that material. Discuss as a class the reasons why each material might have been chosen.

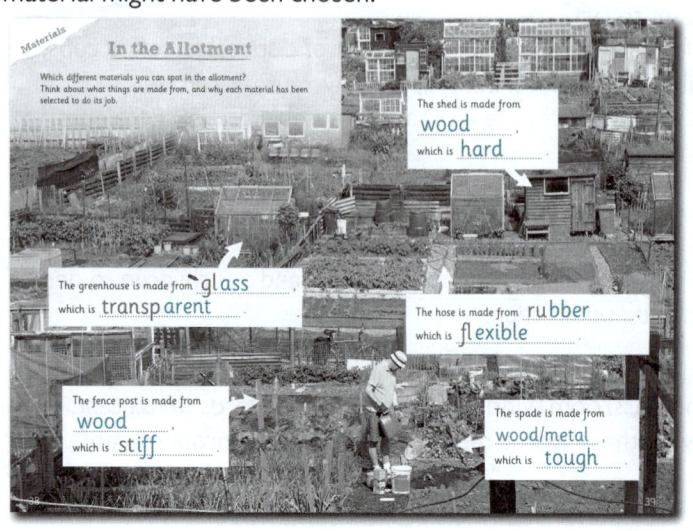

Science Links

A visit to a garden is a chance to reinforce learning from other science topics. For example, it provides opportunities to collect minibeasts, and to observe trees and other plant life.

Key Questions

"What is this made from?"

"How do you think it was made?"

"What does it feel like to touch?"

"Does it bend easily?"

"Do you think this object will last a long time? Why? / Why not?"

Extension Ideas

Look inside the compost bin and take out a sample to investigate. You might want to have some magnifying glasses or bug boxes to hand.

What materials can be composted? How do the materials decompose? What can we do with the compost afterwards?

2. Ask pupils to design their own 'Materials Garden' using ideas from their visit and the information in the Activity Book. Children should aim to include a range of materials for different purposes — for example stone statues, metal climbing frames, a wooden bench, a plastic slide.

   By now they should now be able to explain why they have selected each material, by referencing that material's properties.

   Children might choose different ways to design their garden. They might make a collage, use magazine clippings or even 'junk-model' a 3D garden.

   Pupils might have the opportunity to work independently, in pairs or small groups and should be given time to discuss and note down their ideas before starting.

Extension Ideas

Some children might also like to build on their knowledge of animals and habitats and think about the sort of animals that could live in their garden.

They may have found some mini beasts during their garden visit, which they would like to include images or models of, or they could research the sorts of birds and mammals that are often found living in gardens.

They could then think about what materials the animals could use to build their homes, where they might find a waterproof place to live, or which materials in the garden might be dangerous for animals in some way.

Plenary Questions

1. Tell me some of the things that you have included in your garden.
2. Which materials did you choose?
3. Why did you think that material was suitable?
   What properties does it have that makes it good for the job?

Follow-Up Ideas

1. Play a 'Guess the Material' game. Sit the class in a circle and have a bag prepared containing several everyday items made of different materials. Ask a pupil to reach their hand into the bag, without looking, and describe the object, including some of its properties. Can the rest of the class guess what the object is and what it is made from?

2. Explore some of the materials that animals use to make tools. For example, some chimpanzees make stone hammers, birds make nests out of twigs and feathers, and orangutans make whistles from bundles of leaves. There are some more examples here:
   www.livescience.com/9761-10-animals-tools.html

3. Investigate which ball is the bounciest. Bring in a selection of balls and ask children to predict which one will bounce highest. Introduce the idea of a fair test and which factors need to stay the same (dropped from the same height, with the same amount of force, onto the same surface).
   Record the height of the bounce on a simple bar chart and ask children to discuss the results, with reference to the ball's material and its properties.

Notes on Assessment (Materials)

You'll need to assess pupils' understanding of both the knowledge-based requirements from the Science Programme of Study and the 'Working Scientifically' requirements that underpin the Key Stage 1 curriculum.

The 'Materials' section gives opportunities for pupils to **work scientifically** by:
- Observing closely, using simple equipment.
- Identifying and classifying materials.
- Using their observations and ideas to suggest answers to questions.
- Performing simple tests.
- Gathering and recording data to help in answering questions.

The tasks pupils complete in the **Activity Book** will help you assess pupils' understanding of the 'Materials' section of the Year 1 Programme of Study.

For both the 'Materials' section of the Programme of Study and the 'Working Scientifically' requirements, you can use **Classroom Assessment**.

This will allow pupils who may not have strong literacy skills to demonstrate their understanding practically and verbally.

Year 1 Science Programme of Study: MATERIALS	KS1 Science: Working Scientifically
Distinguish between an object and the material from which it is made / Identify and name a variety of everyday materials, including wood, plastic, glass, metal, water, and rock / Describe the simple physical properties of a variety of everyday materials / Compare and group together a variety of everyday materials on the basis of their simple physical properties	Observing closely, using simple equipment / Identifying and classifying materials / Using their observations and ideas to suggest answers to questions / Performing simple tests / Gathering and recording data to help in answering questions

Classroom Assessment

Classroom Assessment should be in the form of small-group work, observation and the use of open-ended questions. Try focusing on just five or six pupils in each lesson, so you get a deeper understanding of the level they're working at.

Session 1: What's it Made From?

The main skill that is developed through this topic is the ability to identify and classify materials. You can use the whole class work at the beginning of the lesson to gauge which pupils are already relatively skilful and which pupils will need more support over the coming lessons.

During the 'materials treasure hunt', choose a group of pupils to focus on and observe. Notice the range of materials they are able to spot and identify.

Initial Judgements
Which pupils are familiar with a range of materials? Who can describe them using scientific language? Who is beginning to classify materials by noticing similarities and differences?

Y1 Science PoS: MATERIALS	Working Scientifically
✓ ✓	✓ ✓

48 Year 1: Section Four — Materials

Session 2: Talking About Materials

Choose several mixed ability pairs to talk to while the class is working independently. Use open-ended questions to gauge how well pupils are able to describe the properties of materials. With each pair, return to the selection of everyday objects. Ask them to talk to you about their suggestions of which objects are similar somehow and which are different.

Prompt Questions
Did you spot two objects that are the same in some way? Why did you choose those ones? Explain your answer. Which two objects would you say are really different from each other? Why do you think that?

Quick Experiment

The kitchen roll experiment gives pupils a nice opportunity to perform a simple test, as well as gathering some data to help them answer a question. Make a note of which pupils were able to explain their predictions and who demonstrated a good understanding of the test. Who could explain how the results helped them answer a question? You will probably want to do the experiment as a whole class, but you can choose some of your more able children to help measure the water and then encourage them to draw conclusions.

Prompt Questions
Which kitchen roll do you think will be most absorbent? Why?
This kitchen roll soaked up the most water — what does that tell us? Can you tell me more?

Session 3: In the Allotment

The final session in the topic will give you a chance to see which pupils have secured their knowledge about materials. As children are working on their designs you can pick out any children you are unsure about and ask them about their work.

Prompt Questions
Tell me about your garden and the materials you have used. Talk to me about the properties of this material. Why did you choose that? What properties make it good for that job? What else could you have used?

The Follow-Up Activity 'Investigate which ball is the bounciest' provides an opportunity for the pupils to perform a simple test, and gather and record data. Ask pupils to make predictions in advance about which balls will be most/least bouncy. Can they explain their choices in terms of the properties of the materials?

Recording Pupils' Attainment

By the end of the topic, you should be confident in your judgement of which pupils in your class have met the topic's learning objectives. You should also know which pupils are yet to meet the learning objectives and which children have moved beyond the Year One Programme of Study with additional skills and knowledge.

Record pupils' attainment in the Assessment Grid on the CD-ROM. You may wish to use a traffic light system to colour-code the grid.

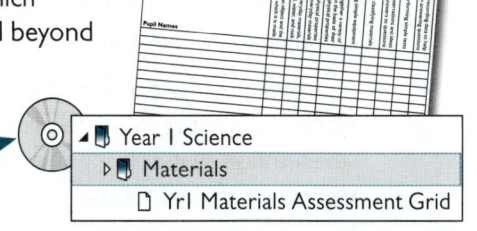

▸ Year 1 Science
  ▸ Materials
    ▫ Yr1 Materials Assessment Grid

Year 1: Section Four — Materials

Year 2: Section One — Living Things
Alive, Dead or Never Lived?

> **Learning Objectives:**
> - To understand the seven life processes that all living things do.
> - To recognise whether something is living, is dead or has never been alive.
> - To understand how animals carry out the seven life processes.
> - To begin to understand how plants carry out the seven life processes.
>
> **Year 2 Science Programme of Study**
> "Explore and compare the differences between things that are living, dead, and things that have never been alive."

Preparation: Prepare a flipchart sheet and 4 different coloured markers. Provide some PE hoops for sorting, and a selection of items that are living, dead and have never lived. (See the Teacher Notes below for some suggestions.)

Lesson Activities

1. Ask the children to tell you whether they think that everyone in the classroom is alive. Of course they will answer "yes!", but how do they know? Allow some time for them to discuss this in pairs and take feedback. For example, they may say that humans grow, breathe, eat, have babies, think etc.

2. Use one of the coloured markers to record all of their ideas on a flipchart, around the words 'Living Things'. Do not correct any misconceptions at this stage.

3. Provide a selection of objects that are living, dead and have never been alive (see the Teacher Notes on the right for some ideas). Ask the children to sort these items into three categories, using the PE hoops and writing labels: 'living', 'dead', 'never lived'. Some of the objects may need explanation — for example, the children may not know that paper comes from wood, which comes from trees. Help them to focus on the materials rather than the objects when it comes to dead/never lived. For example, a leather belt was never alive, but the leather itself was once part of a cow that was alive. Photograph their final results or stick some of the objects onto paper for display.

4. Look at one of the pot plants and ask the children to discuss how they know it is alive. They will probably come up with ideas about how it grows from a seed but may not be able to say much more. Add their ideas to the flipchart using a different colour.

5. Ask questions related to the ideas they gave about humans in point 1. For example, "Do plants move?", "Do plants breathe?", "Can plants talk?"

6. Repeat with one of the invertebrates, using a third colour. Are there any ideas that have come up in each colour?

7. Read the first part of page 2 of the Activity Book together. Explain that the seven things that all living things do are called the 'seven life processes'.

Teacher Notes

Item suggestions for sorting activity:
- *Living* — a variety of pot plants, invertebrates (e.g. snails, woodlice) in pots. Ensure that these are released immediately after the activity.
- *Dead* — fallen leaves, some paper, an empty snail shell, a feather, a leather belt, a wooden ruler, a piece of cotton clothing, a cork.
- *Never lived* — a few stones/pebbles, a plastic spoon, a teddy/toy, a sweet wrapper, a mirror, a piece of synthetic clothing (e.g. a plastic raincoat).

Phonics & Spelling Links

Use the word 'oxygen' in your teaching of 'ge' as a /dʒ/ sound, rather than the usual /g/ sound. Reinforce this by asking children whether they can think of any words that start with 'gen' — e.g. 'general', 'generate'. In fact these words all have the same root from Latin and Greek, meaning 'birth' or 'kind' (hence 'genus').

8. Discuss the seven life processes and how each one relates to humans/other animals. Animals move around, they lay eggs or have babies, which grow into adults, they use their sensory organs to sense the world around them, they get rid of waste by breathing out waste air and going to the toilet, they take oxygen from the air and they get energy from food. Use a fourth colour to circle any of the life processes that they identified on the flipchart and write on any that they did not come up with.

9. Look at the labelled plant picture at the bottom of page 2 of the Activity Book together. Explain that not all of the seven life processes are as easy to spot with plants, but they do still carry out all of these if they are alive. Link each one back to the processes at the top of the page as you read them together.

10. Ask pupils to work through page 3 of the Activity Book and address any misconceptions.

Extension Ideas

You could teach the mnemonic MRS GREN (sometimes given as MRS NERG) to help remember the seven life processes — movement, respiration (using oxygen to get energy from food), sensitivity, growth, reproduction, excretion (getting rid of waste), nutrition. However, these words can be difficult for young children to understand.

Teacher Notes

Plants take in carbon dioxide during the daytime so they can use the sunlight to photosynthesise, but they can also take in oxygen so that their cells can respire to make energy. Some of this oxygen has been produced by the plants during the day. All living things take in oxygen for respiration.

Extension Activity

Discuss some more abstract ideas, e.g. "Is a car alive?" (it does move and uses fuel, which is like food, but it doesn't grow); "Is a piece of fruit alive?" (it's no longer growing on the plant, but if it contains seeds then they could grow into a new plant); "Is a flame alive?" (it uses fuel for food, moves, grows etc. but does not produce offspring). Do not worry if the children don't come up with a definitive answer. It is more important for the children to use scientific language and refer to the seven life processes about which they have been learning.

Plenary Questions

1. What are the seven life processes that prove that something is alive?
2. How can we tell that something is dead?
3. How do we know that something has never lived?

Follow-Up Ideas

1. Go on an 'Alive, Dead or Never Lived?' Scavenger Hunt, using the sheet provided on the CD-ROM. The children will need to be able to attach objects to their sheets (except living animals or buildings!), or they could collect them in bags or trays and stick them on back in the classroom. They will also need pencils to draw any objects that they are unable to collect.

2. Take photographs of children acting out the seven life processes. For example, moving like different animals, growing like a plant, doing actions to show the different senses, holding a baby doll, breathing in oxygen, breathing out waste gas, eating. Use these for a classroom display. You could also play a game where the children have to do the action for the life process you shout out (agree the actions in advance). Anyone who does the wrong action is out.

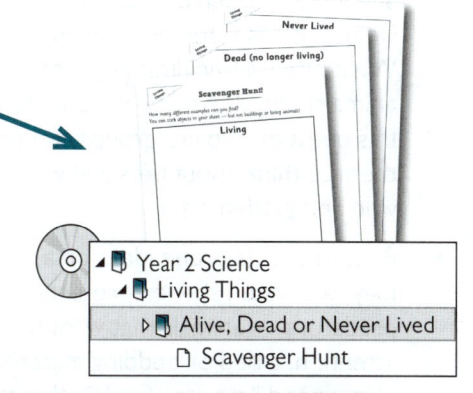

Year 2: Section One — Living Things

Habitats

Learning Objectives:
- To know what a habitat is.
- To begin to understand how habitats provide for the basic needs of the plants and animals that live there.
- To discuss how living things in a habitat depend on each other.

Year 2 Science Programme of Study
"Identify that most living things live in habitats to which they are suited and describe how different habitats provide for the basic needs of different kinds of animals and plants, and how they depend on each other."

Preparation: *Provide a flipchart and some pens, and prepare the habitat slides from the CD-ROM.*

Lesson Activities

1. Discuss the places where children in the class live. They will probably give answers such as 'house' or 'flat'. Ask if they would be able to get everything they needed by staying on their own, only in that place. Discuss the fact that they would need to go outside of the building (e.g. to the shop for food, to school for learning and socialising, outside for fresh air and exercise) and that they depend on other people (e.g. their families).

2. Repeat by asking about a bird — it may sleep in a nest but it also needs to move away from the nest to get food, escape from predators, meet a mate etc.

3. Explain that the place where an animal lives and spends its time is called a 'habitat', and that all living things live in a particular habitat to which they are suited. Briefly discuss some examples of habitats, e.g. deciduous woodland (you may need to recap this term from Year 1), ponds, seashores, deserts, tropical rainforests.

4. Read the first part of page 4 of the Activity Book together. Ask the children to complete the HABITAT acrostic.

5. See if the children can remember the seven life processes from the previous session. What else do living things (plants and animals) need? Ask the children to discuss this question in pairs/groups and encourage them to think about pets and wild animals, wild and garden plants.

6. Record the children's ideas on a flipchart. For example, they may say: water, shelter/protection (from the weather, from predators — animals that want to eat them), air, warmth, love/attention, a bed or bedding material, animals need exercise, plants need light etc. Explain that the right habitat should supply all of a plant's or animal's basic needs.

Phonics & Spelling Links
When teaching the /əl/ sound at the end of words, use the words 'squirrel' and 'animal'. You can't hear the difference when these words are spoken — pupils will just need to learn them!

Extension Activity
Work together as a class to write your own HABITAT acrostic.

7. Talk about the ways in which plants and animals in a particular habitat depend on each other. For example:
   Food — some animals eat plants, some eat other animals, and some eat both (recap the terms 'herbivores', 'carnivores' and 'omnivores' from Year 1 — these will come up again in the next session). Some plants even eat animals (you could show the children photographs or videos of carnivorous plants such as the Venus fly trap, sundew or pitcher plant).
   Shelter — leaves can provide protection from sun or rain and somewhere for animals to hide from predators.
   Pollination and **seed dispersal** — insects such as bees and butterflies help to spread pollen between flowers; animals help to spread seeds further away from the parent plants, e.g. by burying them, by them being stuck to their fur or by eating fruit and the seeds passing undigested through their bodies. (At this stage, children don't need to know the terms 'pollination' and 'seed dispersal', but you can introduce the concepts to them as examples of how plants depend on animals.)

8. Look at the labelled tree picture at the bottom of page 5 of the Activity Book together. Discuss the ways that many animals and other plants depend on the tree. Ask the children, "Did you know that over 280 different species (types) of insects can be found on an oak tree?"

9. Ask the children to work through page 5 of the Activity Book.

Teacher Notes
You can find some information on carnivorous plants at:
www.kew.org/kew-gardens/whats-in-the-gardens/carnivorous-plants

Extension Activity
Can the children tell you how the tree depends on the other plants and animals? For example, if squirrels bury seeds such as acorns, some can be forgotten about and are able to grow into new trees.

Plenary Questions

1. What is a habitat? Can you give an example of a habitat?
2. How do animals and plants in a habitat depend on each other?

Follow-Up Ideas

1. Look at the slides on the CD-ROM that show different habitats. Talk about how some of these are examples of UK habitats and others are from different parts of the world. Can they tell you which are local and which are global? How can they tell?

2. Carry out some Internet research into different habitats from around the world. (BBC Bitesize has a useful list, plus videos and games: www.bbc.co.uk/bitesize/topics/zx882hv.) Can you compile an A-Z of animals in their habitats as a class? You may need to be a bit creative, e.g. "Zebras live in the savannah"!

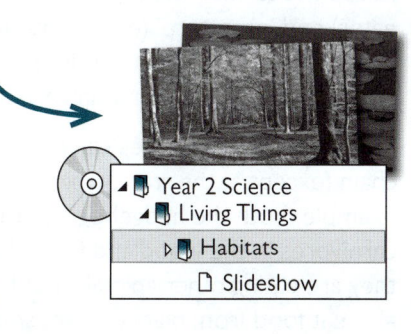

Year 2: Section One — Living Things

Food Chains

> **Learning Objectives:**
> - To understand what a food chain is.
> - To know that all food chains begin with plants.
> - To recap the vocabulary 'carnivore', 'herbivore' and 'omnivore' from Year 1.
>
> **Year 2 Science Programme of Study**
> "Describe how animals obtain their food from plants and other animals, using the idea of a simple food chain, and identify and name different sources of food."

Preparation: Print copies of the 'Food Chain Jigsaw' sheets onto card for pairs/groups to share.

Lesson Activities

1. Recap the work in the previous session about how plants and animals in a habitat depend on each other, particularly for food. Remind the children that all living things need food (referring back to the seven life processes), which provides the energy they need to stay alive.

2. Ask the question: "Do plants eat food?" and allow the children some time to discuss this. Talk about the fact that plants need food but they don't eat it in the way that animals do. (You could ask them to imagine a plant picking up food with its leaves, having a mouth full of teeth or a bulging stomach!)

3. Briefly introduce the fact that plants make their own food using sunlight, water and air (use the term carbon dioxide if you choose to). Tell them that they will be learning more about this in the 'Plants' sessions.

4. Read the top half of pages 6-7 of the Activity Book together:

5. Explain that the arrows in a food chain show which way the energy is going and mean "eaten by".

6. Recap the terms 'herbivore' (plant-eater), 'carnivore' (meat-eater) and 'omnivore' (eats plants and animals). Discuss whether each of the animals in the food chains shown is a carnivore, herbivore or omnivore

7. Point out that omnivores can occur anywhere in the food chain (except at the start, which will always be a plant). For example, both the hedgehog and the fox are acting as carnivores in the woodland food chain in the Activity Book, as they are eating other animals, but both of these animals do also eat food from plants. Also, some food chains are longer than others — compare the grassland and woodland food chains in the Activity Book.

Extension Ideas

You could introduce more detailed vocabulary if you think it is appropriate. For example: 'producer' (plants produce food), 'consumer' (meaning 'one that eats'), 'predator' (an animal that hunts another animal for food) and 'prey' (an animal that is eaten by other animals). However, the children will learn these in Year 4 when they revisit food chains.

Phonics & Spelling Links

Encourage pupils to think about the sense of words like 'hedgehog' (hogs hedges) and 'grasshopper' (hops in the grass). Breaking up the words in this way will help with their spelling.

You could use the word 'grasshopper' when teaching double consonants before '-er'.

Extension Ideas

Can the children suggest some replacements for the plants and animals included in the food chains they have looked at? For example, changing the worm to a beetle or the buzzard to a badger? Do they think these new food chains would still work?

8. Ask the children to work through pages 6-7 of the Activity Book:

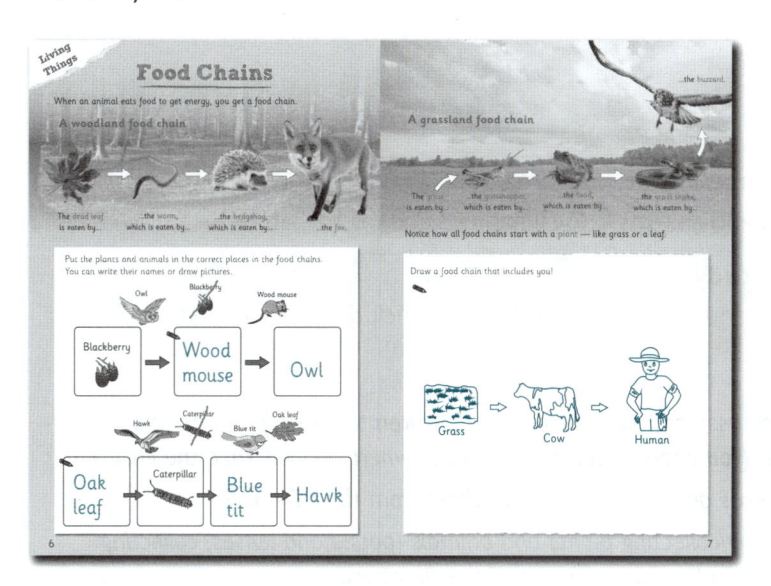

Extension Ideas

Discuss what might happen to the other parts of the food chain if there was a break in the chain — i.e. if one of the organisms dies out or moves away. For example, if all the toads in the grassland food chain died out due to a disease. The grass snake would have to find some other food to eat or they could die out, which would also affect the buzzard. Similarly, the grasshoppers wouldn't be eaten by the toads, so there would be lots more of them, and more grass would be eaten. This will help to reinforce the fact that the plants and animals in a habitat depend on each other.

9. You could give the following examples of simple human food chains to help the children come up with their own:
   grass → cow → human
   algae → shrimp → fish → human
   bread (from wheat) → human
   apple → human

Extension Activity

Children can have a go at creating their own food chains, using real or imaginary plants and animals.

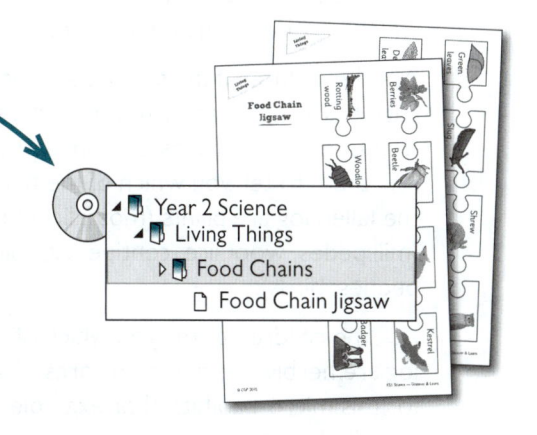

10. As a final activity, cut out and mix up copies of the cards from the 'Food Chain Jigsaws' sheet so that the children can make their own food chains. As long as they start with a plant and end with a large carnivore (indicated by the straight-edged jigsaw pieces), they can experiment with the animals in between. They could work in pairs or small groups and discuss the order of the animals in the chain they have come up with.

Plenary Questions

1. Why do all living things need food?
2. How do plants get their food?
3. What is a herbivore/carnivore/omnivore? Can you give some examples?
4. What is a food chain?
5. What type of living thing is always at the start of a food chain?

Follow-Up Ideas

1. The children can make more of their own food chains, using the plants and animals from the jigsaw cards or by researching others in books or online. Each pupil could be one particular plant or animal, and they could show the links in the food chain by linking hands and standing in a line.

2. Make a 'menu' for a particular habitat, where each section of the menu is a different part of the food chain, beginning with plants as the 'starters'.

3. Split the children into three groups — each with different coloured bands — to represent plants, herbivores and carnivores. Then play a chasing game where the aim is to make mini food chains by grabbing their 'food' around the waist as they run.

Year 2: Section One — Living Things

Micro-habitats

> **Learning Objectives:**
> - To know what a micro-habitat is.
> - To locate habitats and micro-habitats in your local area.
> - To find, identify and name plants and animals in local habitats and micro-habitats.
>
> **Year 2 Science Programme of Study**
> "Identify and name a variety of plants and animals in their habitats, including micro-habitats."

Preparation: Carry out a pre-visit and risk assessment for taking the children to investigate habitats in your school grounds or local area (you need to decide in advance where you will take the children).

Prepare the identification cards and the investigation sheet from the CD-ROM.

Provide equipment for studying/collecting plants and animals (pots, hand lenses, collecting trays/white sheets of fabric or paper, spoons/paintbrushes/pooters).

Lesson Activities

1. Recap the meaning of the term habitat from the earlier session. Then read page 8 of the Activity Book together, which introduces the term 'micro-habitat'.

2. Ask the children if the fallen log in the picture on page 8 is living, dead or never lived, referring back to the seven life processes from a previous lesson. Ask them to tell you which of the things living on the fallen log are plants (moss, lichen) or animals (millipedes, woodlice, centipedes, spiders, slugs, beetles, birds).

3. Ask the children to tell you which of the animals living in/under the log are herbivores and carnivores. Can they construct a food chain for this micro-habitat? (For example, dead wood ➡ millipede, woodlouse ➡ centipede or spider ➡ bird.)

4. Read through page 9 of the Activity Book, and ask the children to complete the activities.

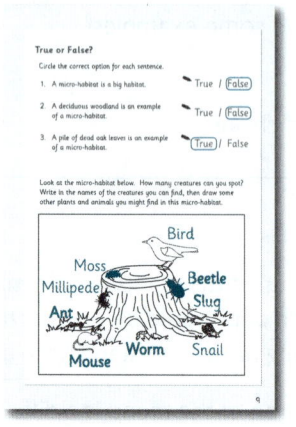

5. Tell the children that you are all going to go outside to explore the habitats and micro-habitats in your school grounds/local area (whichever you have chosen in advance). Organise the children into groups with a set of equipment each and demonstrate how to use the equipment for collecting/observing plants and animals.

Phonics & Spelling Links

Note the differences between the singular and plural forms of woodlouse/woodlice. Compare to mouse/mice. Does the same apply to the plural of house?

You might also like to use 'woodlice' and 'centipede' as examples of words which have 'ce' pronounced /s/.

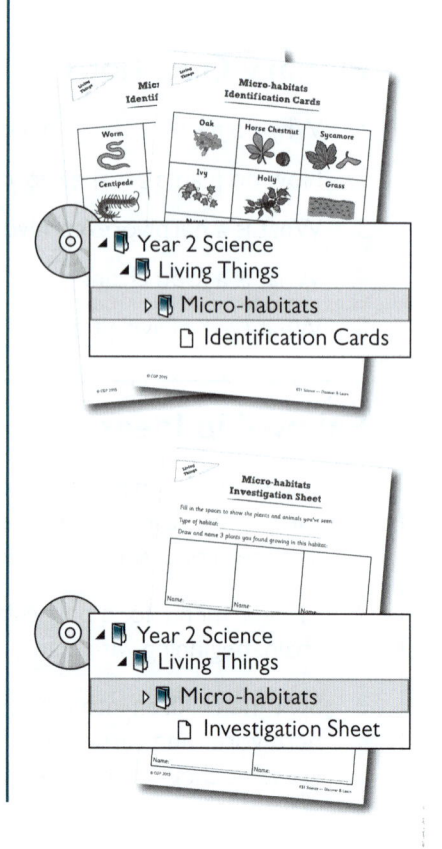

56   *Year 2: Section One — Living Things*

6. Talk about how to show care and respect for plants (not pulling off lots of leaves or trampling vegetation) and animals (collecting/handling them carefully and returning them to the place where they were found). Ensure that each group has access to the identification cards from the CD-ROM and go over the features they can look for (e.g. leaf shape, number of legs) and the names.

7. Look at the micro-habitat Investigation Sheet from the CD-ROM. Explain to the children that they will be looking at a particular local habitat (take ideas from the children about what this habitat might be, e.g. deciduous woodland, urban, field) and that they need to find and identify 3 plants. They will then find a micro-habitat (e.g. a fallen log, under a stone, in a bush) and look for 4 animals. They will be able to use the identification cards to help them. They will then return to the classroom to complete the investigation sheet. (You may decide to also bring leaf samples and invertebrates in pots back into the classroom for the children to study further and draw.)

8. Ask the children to complete the Investigation Sheet, recording the plants and animals that they found.

Plenary Questions

1. What is a habitat? Give an example from your local area.
2. What is a micro-habitat? Give an example from your local area.
3. Which plants did you find locally and where did you find them?
4. Which animals did you find locally and where did you find them?

Teacher Notes
Planning the activity

- *Decide where you are going to carry out the outdoor activity. Ensure that you have a good look around in advance (ideally with the other adults who will be working with the children) to identify any risks/hazards and to check that there is at least one habitat and one micro-habitat for the children to explore. Also look at the identification cards on the CD-ROM and check that you can find at least 3 of the plants and 4 of the animals shown.*
- *If your school grounds are largely paved, with little 'green space', the children can still investigate them as an example of an urban habitat. You should be able to find some plants — even if they are thought of as 'weeds'. There will be invertebrates ('minibeasts') around the edges of the playground, in corners between walls and under rocks or stones.*
- *You could provide micro-habitats for the children to explore by leaving piles of logs, overturned pots, large stones or tubs of long grass in the school grounds. Old pots or washing-up bowls (cleaned with sterilising fluid and hot water) can be used to grow plants. It will require some time for the micro-habitats to become populated, but animals should move in within a week or two.*

Implementing the activity

- *Help the children to lift or roll logs or stones to see what's underneath. Ensure that they don't then walk or sit in the space where the logs/stones were, squashing the animals!*
- *Gently shake bushes or tree branches over a collecting tray or white sheet. Invertebrates will fall down for observation.*
- *Show how to use paintbrushes to brush invertebrates into pots.*
- *Carefully lift sections of bark off fallen logs or tree stumps, but don't encourage the children to do this themselves (it could decimate the micro-habitat!).*
- *If there are any fungi, explain that these may be poisonous, so it's best not to touch them.*
- *Make sure that the children do not put their fingers in their mouths or near their eyes, and that they wash their hands thoroughly after the activity.*

Follow-Up Ideas

1. The children could make collages of the habitats/micro-habitats they observed, and recreate some of the plants and animals that they found.
2. Help the children to create new habitats or micro-habitats in your school grounds.
3. If possible, visit a different habitat or micro-habitat in the local area or further afield, so that the children can compare the plants and animals they found in each one.

The Seashore

> **Learning Objectives:**
> - To find out about a different habitat – the seashore.
> - To learn about some living things from the seashore habitat.
> - To know that a rock pool is a micro-habitat found at the seashore.
>
> **Year 2 Science Programme of Study**
> "Identify and name a variety of plants and animals in their habitats, including micro-habitats. Identify that most living things live in habitats to which they are suited and describe how different habitats provide for the basic needs of different kinds of animals and plants, and how they depend on each other."

Lesson Activities

1. Discuss the seashore and how it is a habitat for different creatures. Ask the pupils what living things they might expect to find at the seashore. Can they think of any micro-habitats here? For example, they may say 'a rock pool' or 'under a rock'.

2. Explain to the children that the seashore can be a difficult place to live, because the tide goes in and out at different times of day. The living things (organisms) at the seashore cope with this in different ways: some animals have shells, some types of seaweed can dry out but still stay alive and organisms choose to live in different parts of the shore (those that like it mainly dry live on the upper shore, those that like it mainly wet live on the lower shore and those that like it dry half the time and wet half the time prefer the middle shore).

3. Look at the top half of pages 10-11 of the Activity Book together.

4. Read the information about each living thing and decide whether it is an animal or a plant (or 'like a plant' — see the Teacher Notes on the right). Focus on barnacles in particular, as children may have seen these before but not realised that they are live animals, as they are clamped to the rocks. Ask the children to recall the seven life processes and go over each one for a barnacle:
   It moves — a hole in the top of the shell opens up when it is covered by saltwater.
   It has babies — these come from eggs.
   It grows — it needs to enlarge its shell as the animal inside gets bigger.
   It feeds — using its legs to collect plankton from the water.
   It senses — using hairs on its legs to detect water levels and danger.
   It gets rid of waste — by pushing it out with its muscles.
   It takes oxygen from the water — this comes in through its shell, and is used by the barnacle to make energy from food.

5. Help the children to compare a rock pool to a pond. The main difference is that rock pools contain saltwater whereas ponds contain freshwater, which means that different types of plants and animals live in them.

Teacher Notes

Although seaweed looks like a plant, it is actually a type of algae. Seaweeds do make their food by photosynthesis (converting energy from sunlight into materials for growth), but they do not have features such as stems, leaves or flowers. However, seaweed plays the same role in food chains as plants.

Extension Ideas

Search online for videos of barnacles feeding to show the children. They will be fascinated! Explain to the children how barnacles mainly feed on plankton — tiny plants and animals which float around underwater. Like seaweed, plankton are usually found at the start of food chains.

6. If you have access to a pond and some equipment (nets, collecting trays/ice cream tubs and identification books/sheets), try some pond dipping. If not, search online for pictures of pond plants and animals. Can the children find any living things that look similar in the two habitats, e.g. common prawn and freshwater shrimp, periwinkle and pond snail, seaweed and pondweed?
7. Ask the children to complete the activities in the Activity Book. You may need to explain to them how to complete the crossword.

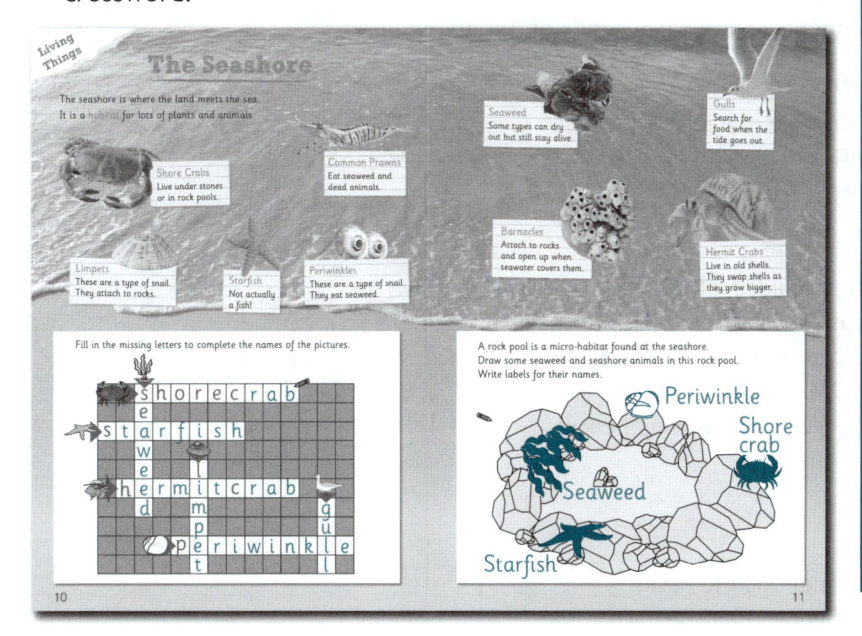

Teacher Notes

You could use the 'Pond Pack' found at www.rbkc.gov.uk/pdf/pond_pack_2010.pdf to help identify different pond plants and animals.

Extension Ideas

As a class, try and come up with some food chains in this habitat. For example:

seaweed ➔ periwinkle ➔ starfish ➔ shore crab

or:

seaweed ➔ limpet ➔ hermit crab ➔ gull

You could also search online for a video of a starfish eating. It will grip its prey with its arms, and then push its stomach outside its body to absorb the food!

Plenary Questions

1. Which habitat have we learnt about?
2. Why is a rock pool an example of a micro-habitat?
3. What living things can be found in the seashore habitat / rock pool micro-habitat?
4. How do these living things depend on each other?

Follow-Up Ideas

1. Print out copies of the sheet 'All Washed Up!' on the CD-ROM. Explain how objects become washed up on the shore when the tide comes in. You could introduce the term 'strandline' as a line of objects that are left behind when the tide goes out — seaweed, animals (dead and alive), human rubbish etc. Ask the children to sort the objects into the buckets labelled 'Living', 'Dead' and 'Never Lived'. They can either draw lines from the objects to the correct buckets or draw the objects inside the buckets. Alternatively, you could enlarge and laminate the pictures of the objects and provide real seaside buckets for the children to sort the objects into.

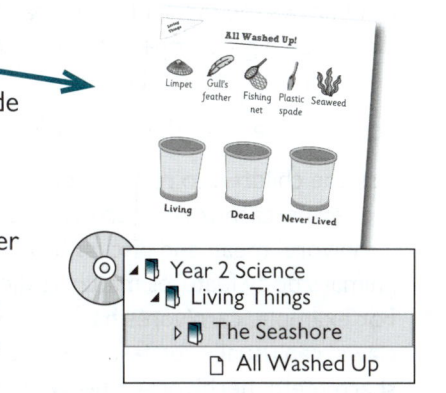

2. Ask the children to imagine they have been on a day trip to the seashore and to write about the living things they found. Encourage them to use the term 'rock pool' and to include the names of some of the seashore plants and animals they have learnt about. This could be done in the form of a postcard — they can then draw a picture on the back to show the seashore.

3. Make textured seashore pictures by mixing sand with paint and PVA glue (and perhaps some glitter for the water). The children can paint the seashore habitat and then print out or draw pictures of seashore animals to stick into the habitat when the paint has dried.

Design a Habitat

*'Design a Habitat' is a **synoptic topic** for the Living Things section. It builds on the concepts introduced in the preceding sessions and applies them to a real-world context.*

Learning Objectives:
- To design a new animal.
- To design a habitat that meets all the basic needs of this animal.

Year 2 Science Programme of Study
"Identify that most living things live in habitats to which they are suited and describe how different habitats provide for the basic needs of different kinds of animals and plants, and how they depend on each other."

Preparation: Prepare some A4 paper folded into 4 rows — enough for groups of 4 children to have a sheet. Print and enlarge copies (to A3) of the 'Pick a Habitat' sheets on the CD-ROM.
Also provide scissors, glue and colouring pencils

Lesson Activities

1. Recap habitats and the fact that they meet all the basic needs of a plant or animal. Tell the children that they are each going to design an animal and then design a habitat for it to live in.

2. Begin by playing the game "Animal Mix-Up" to generate ideas. Each group of 4 children has a sheet of A4 paper folded into 4 equal rows. The first child draws the head of an animal, without the rest of the group seeing, then folds the paper backwards along the fold. They pass it to the next child, who draws half of an animal's body and 2 arms/forelegs, then folds it back. The next child draws the other half of an animal's body and the legs/hind-legs, and the last child draws the tail, folding the paper backwards each time. Finally, each group opens out their paper and looks at their new animal creation. They can then give it a name.

3. Look at page 12 of the Activity Book together.

4. Ask the children to remind you what the terms 'carnivore', 'herbivore' and 'omnivore' mean and discuss how an animal's body features match its diet. For example, carnivores have sharp claws, can usually run fast and have sharp teeth; herbivores have wide, flat teeth and some have large ears to listen out for danger; omnivores will have most of the features of carnivores plus different types of teeth to eat meat and plants.

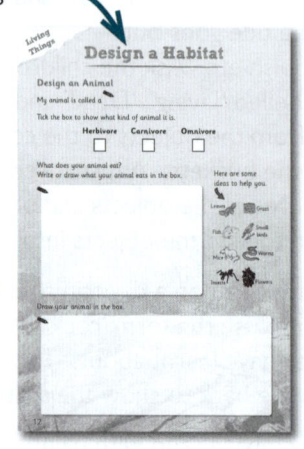

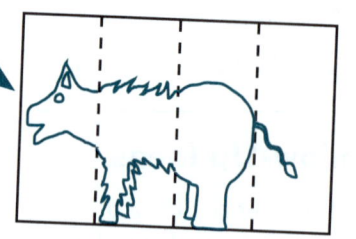

Teacher Notes
You may want to show the children photographs or videos of carnivores, herbivores and omnivores to give them ideas for their own animal designs. For example:
Carnivores: dog, cat, shark, snake, frog, owl, spider, ladybird, centipede.
Herbivores: rabbit, cow, horse, parrot, snail, sheep, elephant, tortoise, giraffe.
Omnivores: squirrel, pig, badger, magpie, fox, hedgehog, robin, ant, bear.

60 Year 2: Section One — Living Things

5. Ask the children to complete page 12 of the Activity Book. They can discuss their ideas with a partner. If their animal eats different food from the choices available, they can draw their own pictures.

6. Tell the children that they are now going to design a habitat for their animal, which will supply all of its basic needs. Allow some time for them to discuss the needs of animals (in pairs/groups) and then take feedback and record their ideas. Ensure that your list includes food, shelter and a (safe/comfortable) place to sleep.

7. Look at page 13 of the Activity Book together and then ask the children to complete it.

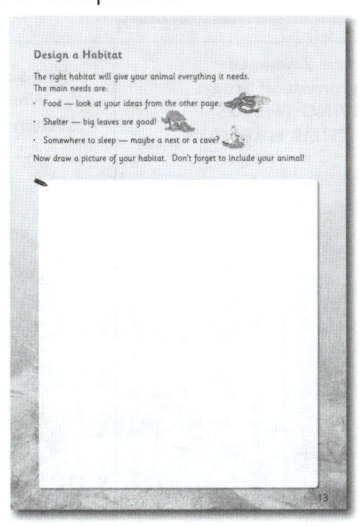

Extension Ideas
Encourage children to choose more specific plants and animals as foods, based on what they found in their local habitat, e.g. oak tree leaves, forget-me-not flowers, woodlice. Early finishers can write sentences about their animals.

Extension Ideas
The children can add other animals into their habitats, perhaps some large carnivores if their animal is a herbivore, or some small invertebrates ("minibeasts"). They can then use the plants and animals in their habitat to create food chains.

Plenary Questions

1. Why is it important for an animal to live in the right habitat?
2. How does your habitat provide food for your animal?
3. How does your habitat provide shelter for your animal?
4. Where will your animal sleep in its new habitat?

Follow-Up Ideas

1. The children can make shoe-box models of their new habitats, with clay models of their animals inside. They could collect real leaves, pebbles etc. from outside in the school grounds.

2. The children can use the 'Pick a Habitat' sheets from the CD-ROM to match the animals to the correct habitats (deciduous woodland, tropical rainforest, ocean or pond). To help them decide, encourage the children to look at the body shapes of the animals, and to consider which animals and habitats would be found in the UK or abroad.

Correct answers:
Deciduous woodland — woodpecker, shrew, blue tit, caterpillar, squirrel, owl, badger, fox, hedgehog. (They may also put water animals in the stream.)
Tropical rainforest — sloth, parrot, giant millipede, anaconda, tree frog, lemur, jaguar.
Ocean — shark, starfish, killer whale, seal, clown fish, lobster, crab.
Pond — tadpole, frog, newt, diving beetle, heron.

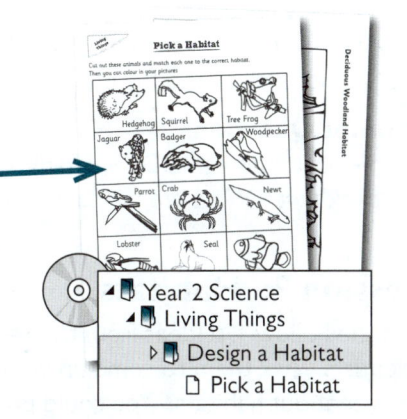

Year 2: Section One — Living Things

Notes on Assessment (Living Things)

You'll need to assess pupils' understanding of both the knowledge-based requirements from the Science Programme of Study and the 'Working Scientifically' requirements that underpin the Key Stage 1 curriculum.

The 'Living Things' section gives opportunities for pupils to **work scientifically** by:
- Asking simple questions and recognising that they can be answered in different ways.
- Observing closely, using simple equipment.
- Identifying and classifying.
- Using their observations and ideas to suggest answers to questions.

The tasks pupils complete in the **Activity Book** will help you assess pupils' understanding of the 'Living Things and their Habitats' section of the Year 2 Programme of Study.

For both the 'Living Things and their Habitats' section of the Programme of Study and the 'Working Scientifically' requirements, you can use **Classroom Assessment**.

This will allow pupils who may not have strong literacy skills to demonstrate their understanding practically and verbally.

Classroom Assessment

Classroom Assessment should be in the form of small-group work, observation and the use of open-ended questions. Try focusing on just five or six pupils in each lesson, so you get a deeper understanding of the level they're working at.

Session 1: Alive, Dead or Never Lived?

In this lesson children are asked to closely observe a range of items in order to answer the question 'Are they living, dead or have they never lived?' Choose a mixed ability group to observe and listen to their discussions. What reasons do they give for their suggestions? Are they able to make links between the objects they are looking at and the more abstract concepts they are investigating?

Prompt Questions
Tell me about this item. Do you think it is living, dead or has it never lived? Why do you think that? What are the clues? Does anybody disagree with that suggestion?

Session 2: Habitats

Use the Follow-Up Ideas from this session to work with your more able scientists. Ask them to come up with some questions they would like to answer about habitats. You could provide these sentence starters:
"I wonder which animal..." / "I want to know which plant/animal lives in..." / "I want to find out more about...".
They can then use reference books, the CD-ROM slideshow and the suggested website to research and answer their own questions.

Session 3: Food Chains

This lesson provides a good opportunity to work with less able pupils to help them secure some of the key information from this topic. Support them as they complete their individual work (although consider doing this as a group, with you scribing to allow more time for discussion) and then work as a group to complete the food chain jigsaws task. Which pupils demonstrate a good understanding of different kinds of animals? Who understands the relationship between an animal and its habitat? Who can put a food chain together in a meaningful way?

Session 4: Micro-habitats

This lesson gives pupils a valuable opportunity to observe plants and animals in a real life setting, using simple equipment. Try to observe as many pupils as possible as they move around their environment. Who is using the equipment correctly? Who is choosing appropriate things to observe? Who is able to note their findings and observations on their sheet?

Prompt Questions
Tell me about what you have been looking at. What have you noticed? What does that tell you about the plant/animal? Can you show me what you have recorded?

Session 5: The Seashore

In this lesson pupils will compare the plants and animals in a pond to those in a rock pool. Some pupils may be able to draw on their existing knowledge and the resources you have provided to identify and classify the different living things. Towards the end of the lesson, choose several mixed ability pairs to talk with and assess how well they have met these learning objectives.

Prompt Questions
Tell me about some similarities you have noticed between a pond and a rock pool. What are the differences? I wonder why the seashore is a habitat. Tell me about some of the plants and animals that live there. How do they rely on each other?

Session 6: Design a Habitat

Look at your Assessment Grid and notice where the gaps are. If there is one particular objective that lots of pupils haven't met, you might like to make that a focus of the lesson. As children are designing their habitats, use this time to talk to children with more gaps in their knowledge and skills and work with them to move their learning forwards.

Intervention
Ask children to describe their habitat to you, but focus on any learning objectives that they have not secured. For example, you might like to discuss the sorts of food chains that could exist in their habitat or what things in their habitat are alive, dead or have never lived.

Recording Pupils' Attainment

By the end of the topic, you should be confident in your judgement of which pupils in your class have met the topic's learning objectives. You should also know which pupils are yet to meet the learning objectives and which children have moved beyond the Year Two Programme of Study with additional skills and knowledge.

Record pupils' attainment in the Assessment Grid on the CD-ROM. You may wish to use a traffic light system to colour-code the grid.

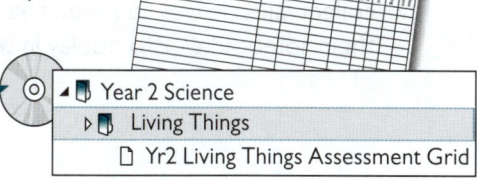

▲ Year 2 Science
▷ Living Things
   Yr2 Living Things Assessment Grid

Year 2: Section One — Living Things

Year 2: Section Two — Plants
A Plant Adventure!

> **Learning Objectives:**
> - To understand what a plant is and what it needs to grow.
> - To carefully observe plants and their different parts.
> - To be able to identify and name some common types of plant.
>
> **Year 2 Science Programme of Study**
> "Observe and describe how seeds and bulbs grow into mature plants. Find out and describe how plants need water, light and a suitable temperature to grow and stay healthy."

Preparation: For this lesson you will need to plan a field trip to somewhere where you can observe a wide range of plants. This could be as simple as somewhere in your local environment where there are trees and wild flowers growing, or you could arrange to visit a local nursery or botanical gardens. On the trip, children will need notebooks, a selection of drawing and painting materials, a digital camera and a handheld magnifying glass or microscope.

Field Trip

1. Explain to the class that they will be going on a field trip, where they will be carefully observing different plants. In particular, they will be noticing:

   a. How plants grow — can they spot plants in different stages of growth, from seeds and bulbs to tiny shoots and large plants with thick stems and many leaves?

   b. What plants need to grow — what are the plants getting from their environment that helps them change from seeds, to small plants and eventually to large plants?

2. On your field trip, give children as much access as possible to a range of plants. Depending on the location they might be able to dissect some samples, and should be allowed to carefully touch specimens and look at them under a magnifying glass or microscope to notice details such as veins in leaves and root systems.

3. If you are visiting your local area you might want to bring a selection of field guides, so that children can have a go at identifying plants.

4. Children could also bring science notebooks and a selection of drawing or painting materials with them to make sketches of the different plants they see. They can then label the plants and their different parts. They could also collect fallen leaves and seed heads to stick in their notebooks or to display in the classroom.

Teacher Notes
Before you go on your field trip remind children of the adage, 'take only photographs, leave only footprints'. It is important that they only collect parts of plants that are dead or fallen. Living plants can be sketched or photographed. Make sure you remind children to take any litter home with them.

Teacher Notes
Some pupils may already have an idea of what plants need, but all pupils should be encouraged to think about this. Is there a gardener watering the plants, or do they get water from rainfall? Are they out in the sun, or under special lights? Is anything added to the soil to encourage growth? What is the temperature like?

Exactly what is needed for seeds and plants to grow will be covered in future sessions, but this is a good opportunity for pupils to begin to discover these things for themselves.

Extension Activities
Depending on the location of your field trip and the time of year, you could also have a go at some other outdoors activities such as:

- *Collecting wild blackberries.*
- *Playing conkers.*
- *Exploring a fallen tree and what else is growing or living inside it.*
- *Investigate the plants that are growing in a pond or by water.*
- *Build a den out of fallen branches and leaves.*

Back in the Classroom

1. Ask children to think about the question: 'What is a plant?' Encourage them to use their observations from the field trip to help answer this question.

2. Share ideas and note that plants are living things. They have roots in the ground, which absorb water and nutrients, and green leaves that absorb air and light to make food. Plants often flower or produce fruit. Parts of different plants can be eaten to provide energy for animals including humans.

3. Read page 14 of the Activity Book as a class. This should help bring together and confirm the pupils' observations from the field trip and their answers to the question 'what is a plant?'. It will remind pupils of the parts of a plant and introduce the idea that they grow from seeds and bulbs.

4. The information given can also be used to help pupils think about what plants need to grow (air, sunlight, water etc...). How did the plants they observed on their field trip get these things from their environment? Discuss this together as a class, encouraging them to try and remember what they saw.

5. Ask the pupils to complete the activities on page 15 of the Activity Book. For the second activity, they could draw one of the favourite plants that they saw on the trip.

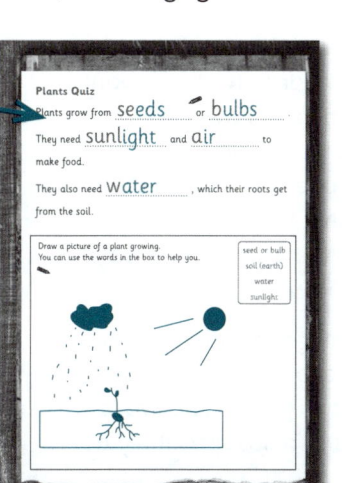

Teacher Notes

Pupils should be familiar with plants and their structure from Year 1, but it is a good idea to discuss this again now to refresh their memories and fill in any gaps in their knowledge.

Extension Activity

Encourage the children to use the correct names to label each part of the plants they are drawing — roots, leaves, flowers etc.

Plenary Questions

1. What was your favourite plant that we saw on our adventure?

2. Were there any places where there were no plants growing? Why could that be?

3. When you visit an outdoor space, what do you need to do to make sure you look after the plants?

Follow-Up Ideas

1. Why not make a display of children's paintings, photographs and a nature table, so that they can explore some of the items that were collected?

2. Ask children to bring in seeds and dried beans from home and have a go at making seed mosaics. There are some instructions here:
www.firstpalette.com/Craft_themes/Food/Seed_Mosaic/Seed_Mosaic.html

3. Place cut flowers in water mixed with food colouring as a visual way of learning how water travels up the stem of a plant. There are instructions here:
theimaginationtree.com/2013/03/dyed-flowers-science-experiment.html

From Acorn to Oak

Learning Objectives:
- To describe how a seed grows into a tree.
- To know what a tree needs to grow and be healthy.

Year 2 Science Programme of Study
"Observe and describe how seeds and bulbs grow into mature plants. Find out and describe how plants need water, light and a suitable temperature to grow and stay healthy."

Preparation: For this lesson you will need one (or several) acorns for the class to look at. If you have access to nearby oak trees you may also want to bring in some examples of leaves and fallen branches to share.

Each child will need a copy of the comic strip sheet, and for less able children you can print and cut out a set of the oak tree cards for them to order and stick down.

Lesson Activities

1. Show the class an acorn. Pass it around for each pupil to examine. Ask the children to think about what it is, what it will become and how it will grow. Recap the observations from the field trip in the previous session — where does this fit into the different stages of growth that the class observed? What do the children think the acorn might look like as it grows and changes?

2. Introduce the scientific term 'germination'. This refers to the point that the acorn sprouts, and the first part of the plant begins to grow. This word is used for all types of seeds and bulbs sprouting, not just acorns.

3. Show this time lapse clip of an acorn germinating and growing into an oak sapling:
www.youtube.com/watch?v=ZK4LjURtaDw

4. Read pages 16-17 of the Activity Book, which look at the different stages of growth of an oak tree. Ask the children to complete the activities independently.

Extension Question

You could ask pupils (or pupils may ask you) the question, 'how do acorns grow underground when there is no light?' (They should remember from the previous session how plants need sunlight to be able to grow.)

Acorns and other seeds and bulbs can grow underground because they have energy stored inside them, which they use as food. When they germinate and the new plant pokes out of the soil, they begin to make their own food from the sunlight, in order to grow healthy and strong.

Teacher Notes

Pupils may be interested to learn about the life cycle of a tree in a little more detail:

Acorn — The seed of an oak tree is called an acorn. Acorns may be buried by squirrels, which helps the trees to grow in new places.

Sprout — The acorn germinates and sends out shoots.

Sapling — The sprout grows taller and grows many leaves.

Mature Tree — The fully grown tree produces fruits that contain seeds.

Snag — A tree can die as a result of disease, lightning, animal damage, drought and old age. Dead trees can provide important habitats for other plants and animals.

Note that the concept of life cycles is covered in more detail in the 'Animals' section of this book. You can choose to introduce the term here, or wait until it is covered later on.

5. Explain that the children are now going to make a comic strip about how an acorn grows into an oak tree. You can find the resources for this activity on the CD-ROM:

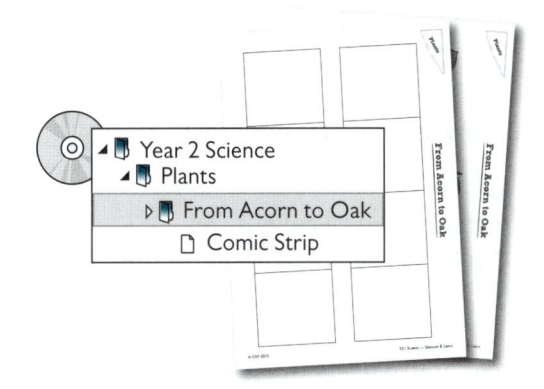

6. Model drawing the first two or three boxes and do some shared writing with the class to come up with captions and speech bubbles.

7. In the first box you could have an acorn underground saying, 'it's dark down here, I can't wait to sprout and see some sunshine'. In the next box the acorn might have sprouted and could say, 'now I'm a big sprout I need plenty of water and sunshine to keep me healthy'.

8. Children will complete their own comic strips to show the complete life cycle of an oak tree. They should include each different phase, as well as information about what the seed and tree need to grow and other events such as producing acorns and losing leaves in autumn.

Teacher Notes

- *More able children can complete the comic strip independently, including as much information as possible. The template has boxes for up to 8 images/captions.*
- *For less able children there are 5 pictures, which you can print and cut out for them to order and add a caption or label to.*
- *For all pupils, it might be worth recapping the different parts of an oak tree to ensure children draw them accurately:*

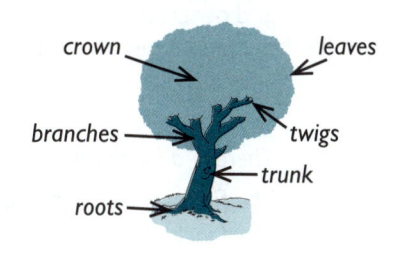

Extension Activity

Look again at the different stages in the life cycle of a tree. Get the class to act out each part — curl up in a tiny ball to be an acorn, slowly uncurl as they sprout, grow gradually taller into a sapling, then extend arms and hands and lift up head to become a mature tree. Can they think of an action to show the tree dying and turning into a snag? You could show the video clip from the previous page again to help them visualise each part that should be acted out.

Plenary Questions

1. Ask the children to share their comic strips with a partner and check that they have included each stage of the life cycle.
2. What are the different stages in the life cycle of an oak tree?
3. Why is important that an oak tree produces acorns?

Follow-Up Ideas

1. Ask pupils to find a tree in their local area. Can they find out what the seeds look like? Can they find some examples of seeds and leaves on the ground? (This will depend on what time of year it is.)
2. Why not have a go at making your own time-lapse video? Cress seeds growing on wet tissue paper would make a simple project.
3. Read the book 'How a Seed Grows' by Helene Jordan, which shows how an acorn grows into an oak tree.
4. If you have managed to acquire a large number of acorns, there are some nice maths activities that you can do with them, such as the ones suggested here:
   livingmontessorinow.com/2012/09/27/outdoor-acorn-math-activities/

What Seeds Need

> **Learning Objectives:**
> - To investigate similarities and differences in seeds and bulbs.
> - To understand what seeds and bulbs need to grow.
> - To carry out an investigation to see how light affects how seeds and plants grow.
>
> **Year 2 Science Programme of Study**
> "Observe and describe how seeds and bulbs grow into mature plants. Find out and describe how plants need water, light and a suitable temperature to grow and stay healthy."

Preparation: *There is a lot to do in this lesson, so you might want to split it into two parts:*

The first, shorter part requires a number of seeds and bulbs to observe. These could include edible seeds such as poppy and sunflower seeds, and tree seeds such as acorns and even a coconut.

For the second part, you will need seeds to plant, as well as paper cups, compost and access to water. Each child will need a copy of the investigation sheet that accompanies this lesson.

Lesson Activities — Part 1

1. Sit the class in a circle and pass round a selection of seeds and bulbs for pupils to observe. You may want to have them work in pairs with magnifying glasses — or if you have access to a digital microscope, you could use this to look closely at each seed before passing it around.

2. Ask children to talk in pairs about what they have been observing. What do they think they are? What do they notice about them? Are any similar? Are any different?

3. Ask the pairs to explain their ideas to the class. Reinforce the fact that plants grow from seeds and bulbs, which can come in many different shapes and sizes.

4. Now ask the pupils to think about what seeds might need in order for them to germinate. In groups, they should write down as many ideas as they can. Once they've had time to do this, collect all of the different ideas by writing them on the whiteboard. The 'correct' answers are: warmth, water and air. If the pupils did not come up with any of these, then you could play 'Hangman' to try and get them to guess the correct words.

5. Explain how germinated plants need some extra things to be able to continue to grow big and strong. These are light (from the Sun) and nutrients (from the soil). Did the pupils come up with these ideas in the previous activity? If not, you could play Hangman again to elicit the correct responses.

Teacher Notes

Seeds are like the embryo of a plant. They disperse and grow into completely new plants each year.

Bulbs are planted in the ground and then continue to multiply each year, making more and more new plants.

As well as growing from seeds or bulbs, some plants can grow from runners, tubers or cuttings, among other things.

Teacher Notes

If pupils are struggling to come up with any ideas, suggest that they think about previous sessions. What did they observe on the field trip, and what can they remember about how acorns grow into oak trees?

Extension Ideas

Can anyone think of things that might stop seeds from growing? Poor soil, seeds being sown too deep, too much or too little water, frozen ground and animals eating them can all stop seeds from germinating.

6. Read pages 18-19 of the Activity Book together, and ask the pupils to complete the activities independently.

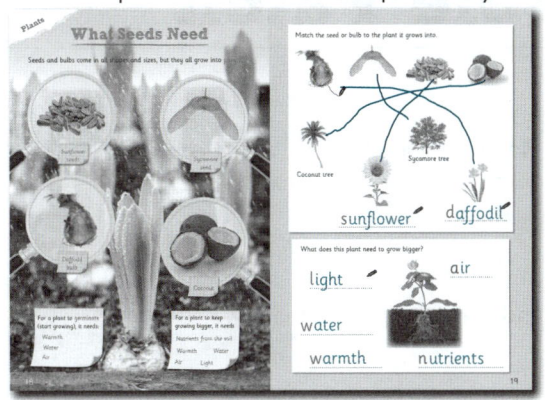

Lesson Activities — Part 2

1. Explain that you are now going to investigate the question: "Do seeds grow best when it is light or dark?" Ask pupils to make a prediction. What do they think is the answer to the question? Why do they think this? You could use a 'think, pair, share' activity — the pupils think about the question themselves, then discuss their ideas in pairs. Then choose a few pairs to explain their conclusions to the class.

2. You can choose which seeds to plant; broad beans, peas and tomato seeds are good options. Demonstrate how to sow a seed and talk about the things you are keeping the same — the same type of seed, type and quantity of compost (both below and above the seed), amount of water, whether you add liquid plant food etc. The only thing that will be different is whether you place the seed in light or dark.

3. Ask the children to work in pairs or small groups to sow two seeds. Each group should place one seed on a light windowsill and one in a dark cupboard. Give each child a print-out of the investigation sheet from the CD-ROM for support.

Teacher Notes

This lesson lays the foundations for planning a fair test. There are three key things to focus on:

- *Make sure the class knows which question you are trying to answer — have it clearly displayed on the whiteboard.*
- *The thing that will change in your investigation is whether it is light or dark. (This is the 'variable', although you don't need to use this word at this stage.)*
- *Everything else must stay the same to make sure the investigation is 'fair'.*

Extension Ideas

This investigation is designed to test the effect of light on how well a plant grows. The more able pupils could now begin to think about the other things a plant needs: warmth, water, nutrients and air. Can they think of an experiment that would test the effect of these different things? For example, testing the effect of temperature by putting one plant in a really cold area, one in a really warm area and one at room temperature.

Plenary Questions

1. What are some of the things that a seed or bulb needs to grow into a plant?
2. What is the thing that we are changing in our investigation? What are some of the factors that we are keeping the same?
3. Do you think the seeds will grow best in the light or dark? Why?

Follow-Up Ideas

1. Pupils should carefully observe the seeds at least once a week and fill in their investigation sheet by drawing a picture of one of the seeds in the light and one in the dark. More able pupils might note any differences underneath. Don't forget to regularly water the seeds and remind children that both sets must receive the same amount of water to keep the test fair.

2. Return to this investigation in a future session and discuss which seeds did better and why that might be. Refer back to the prediction they made — was their prediction correct?

Your Vegetable Patch

> 'Your Vegetable Patch' is a **synoptic topic** for the Plants section. It builds on the concepts introduced in the preceding sessions and applies them to a real-world context.
>
> ### Learning Objectives:
> - To observe how a seed grows into a plant.
> - To understand that plants need water, light and warmth to stay healthy.
>
> ### Year 2 Science Programme of Study
> "Observe and describe how seeds and bulbs grow into mature plants. Find out and describe how plants need water, light and a suitable temperature to grow and stay healthy."

Preparation: This session follows on from 'What Seeds Need'. In pairs or small groups, pupils will have planted two seeds and placed one in light conditions and one in the dark. They will have taken regular observations and noticed how the growth differs between the different conditions. If the plants haven't grown enough for there to be a noticeable difference, wait two more weeks before continuing with this lesson.

Lesson Activities — Part 1

1. Place all of the plants that have been growing in the light on one side of the classroom and the plants that have been in the dark on the other. Ask the children to talk in small groups about what they notice.

2. Each group should describe their observations — the plants that have been in the light should be strong, healthy and green, whereas the plants that have been in the dark should be weedy and yellow.

3. Ask the pupils to think about how they can tell whether a plant is healthy or not. They should refer to their observations to describe the physical features of the plants that were in the dark, and how this shows that the plant has not grown to be strong and healthy. They should compare this to the appearance of the healthy plants which grew in the light.

4. Now ask the pupils to complete their investigation sheets from the previous session by filling in the last observation box and conclusion.

5. Show the class this clip of plants growing:
   www.bbc.co.uk/programmes/p0118qs0
   They will be fascinated to see the plants growing with the process sped up. The clip has no narration, so a nice activity would be for members of the class to describe what is being shown as the video is playing — you want them to be able to use what they have learnt from previous sessions to explain how plants need air, water, warmth, food (nutrients) and sunlight in order to grow healthily. You can pause on the images of rainfall, sunshine and soil, which can be pointed out as prompts to help them to do this.

Teacher Notes

Etiolation is the scientific term for plants that grow without access to light. The plants typically have longer, thinner stems, have smaller leaves and will be yellow in colour.

Extension Ideas

The video clip could provide other prompts for further investigation and discussion. The image of a cactus could lead to questions about how they get the water they need in such a dry environment. The insects shown are also important to the plants' life cycles — they act as pollinators, helping plants to reproduce. This could lead to an investigation of other methods of seed dispersal and how new plants are created.

Lesson Activities — Part 2

1. Explain to the pupils that they are now going to design their own vegetable patch and write instructions for how to care for it using everything they have learned from the topic.

2. To support this part of the lesson you might want to bring in seed catalogues and fliers from garden centres. You could also talk first about children's favourite fruits, vegetables and flowers to give them some ideas of the sorts of things they might plant.

3. Pupils should now use pages 20-21 of the Activity Book to complete their designs:

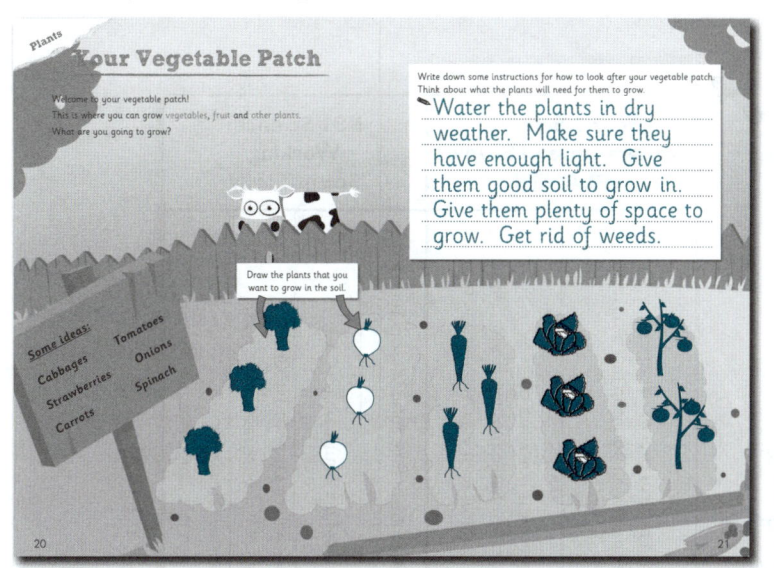

Teacher Notes

Pupils should now be familiar with the things that plants (including vegetables) need in order to grow healthy and strong. They should use this knowledge to help them write the instructions for how to care for their planted vegetables.

Some pupils may like to know a bit more about the different things plants need:

Air — Plants take in oxygen and carbon dioxide from the air. They then produce oxygen, which animals need to survive.

Water — Plants take in water from the soil using their roots. Water helps keep the plants strong — without it, the plants will wilt.

Nutrients — Plants get nutrients from the soil they grow in. It can be a good idea to add 'plant food' to the soil, to ensure they get all the nutrients they need.

Light — Plants use light from the Sun to get the energy they need to make food.

Warmth — Cold temperatures can slow growth and cause damage to plants.

Extension Activity

Pupils could get creative by designing larger vegetable patches. They could use paint or make a collage on a larger sheet of paper. This could then be used for a class display.

Plenary Questions

1. If you have a house plant, where might be a good place to keep it? Why?
2. Why do people often water their gardens during the summer?
3. Why might some gardeners grow their fruits and vegetables in a greenhouse?

Follow-Up Ideas

1. Move the plants that were kept in darkness into the light and continue to water them. Ask the pupils to predict whether they will be able to recover and become strong and healthy. Continue to observe growing plants and notice any changes. Healthy plants can either be sent home or re-potted outside. This is especially nice if you have chosen to grow flowering or edible plants that can be harvested later.

2. You could investigate plants that can grow in very low light:
www.buzzle.com/articles/indoor-plants-that-dont-need-sunlight.html
Or in very dry conditions:
www.buzzle.com/articles/sahara-desert-plants.html

3. In a literacy lesson, children could write instructions on how to grow a seed. In an art lesson, they could design a poster showing how to look after their vegetable gardens. Another nice activity would be for the pupils to work in groups to create short presentations on how to help plants grow.

4. As the plants continue to grow, children can measure their stems, count their leaves or even trace the leaves onto squared paper to calculate their areas.

Notes on Assessment (Plants)

You'll need to assess pupils' understanding of both the knowledge-based requirements from the Science Programme of Study and the 'Working Scientifically' requirements that underpin the Key Stage 1 curriculum.

> The 'Plants' section gives opportunities for pupils to **work scientifically** by:
> - Observing closely, using simple equipment.
> - Performing simple tests.
> - Using their observations and ideas to suggest answers to questions.
> - Gathering and recording data to help in answering questions.

The tasks pupils complete in the **Activity Book** will help you assess pupils' understanding of the 'Plants' section of the Year 2 Programme of Study.

For both the 'Plants' section of the Programme of Study and the 'Working Scientifically' requirements, you can use **Classroom Assessment**.

This will allow pupils who may not have strong literacy skills to demonstrate their understanding practically and verbally.

Year 2 Science Programme of Study: PLANTS	KS1 Science: Working Scientifically
Observe and describe how seeds and bulbs grow into mature plants / Find out and describe how plants need water, light and a suitable temperature to grow and stay healthy	Observing closely, using simple equipment / Performing simple tests / Using their observations and ideas to suggest answers to questions / Gathering and recording data to help in answering questions

Classroom Assessment

Classroom Assessment should be in the form of small-group work, observation and the use of open-ended questions. Try focusing on just five or six pupils in each lesson, so you get a deeper understanding of the level they're working at.

Session 1: A Plant Adventure!

This lesson requires children to closely observe a range of living plants, using magnifying glasses and other equipment. They can then use their observations to have a go at answering the question, 'What is a plant?' Which pupils are able to use the equipment? Who can tell you what they have noticed about the plants they have been looking at? Who uses their observations when answering the question?

Prompt Questions
What is a plant? Tell me something you observed that made you think that? Can you explain your answer? What else did all the plants you saw have in common?

Y2 Science PoS: Plants		Working Scientifically		
Observe and describe how seeds and bulbs grow into mature plants	Find out and describe how plants need water, light and a suitable temperature to grow and stay healthy	Observing closely, using simple equipment	Performing simple tests	Using their observations and ideas to suggest answers to questions	Gathering and recording data to help in answering questions
✓	✓	✓		✓	✓

Year 2: Section Two — Plants

Session 2: From Acorn to Oak

This is a good lesson for children to demonstrate their knowledge of plants, life cycles and how things grow. Work with some of your less able scientists to make sure they have met the main knowledge objectives of this topic. Work as a guided group to order the pictures of an oak tree at different stages and add captions. You could use the Extension Activities to reinforce the different stages of growth and to talk about what plants need at each stage to stay healthy.

Intervention
The most important concepts for your less able pupils to grasp are that an oak tree grows from an acorn, and what it needs in order to grow into a mature tree.

Session 3: What Seeds Need

The practical part of this lesson allows pupils to have a go at planning and carrying out a simple test — sowing two seeds to see if they grow best in the light or the dark. Focus on your more able scientists and use the teacher notes about fair testing and Extension Ideas to generate discussion about how their test will help them to answer the question.

Prompt Questions
Explain to me what will happen once you have sown the seeds. What will that tell us? I wonder what will happen. How will you know if your prediction is right or not? What are you keeping the same in your test? Why is that important?

Session 4: Your Vegetable Patch

In this lesson the pupils will reflect on their tests and the data they have collected. The data could be in the form of actual measurements, or it could be a series of photos, or simply comparing the two groups of plants. Discuss how it can be used to decide whether seeds grow best in the light or the dark. As children are completing their vegetable patch designs, call up a few mixed ability pairs and talk to them about what they have found out. Who is able to link the data they have gathered with answering the question?

Prompt Questions
Tell me what you found out by doing this experiment. Was that what you expected to happen? Why do you think the plants grew better in the light? If we were to do the test again, would you do anything differently to make it better?

Recording Pupils' Attainment

By the end of the topic, you should be confident in your judgement of which pupils in your class have met the topic's learning objectives. You should also know which pupils are yet to meet the learning objectives and which children have moved beyond the Year Two Programme of Study with additional skills and knowledge.

Record pupils' attainment in the Assessment Grid on the CD-ROM. You may wish to use a traffic light system to colour-code the grid.

- Year 2 Science
  - Plants
    - Yr2 Plants Assessment Grid

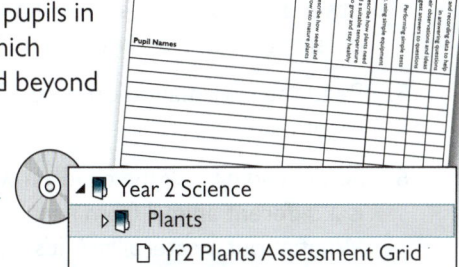

Year 2: Section Two — Plants

Year 2: Section Three — Animals
Life Cycles

> **Learning Objectives:**
> - To understand that animals, including humans, have offspring.
> - To recognise a variety of animal life cycles.
>
> **Year 2 Science Programme of Study**
> "Notice that animals, including humans, have offspring which grow into adults."

Preparation: Children will need whiteboards and pens.
You may want to have access to the Internet.

Lesson Activities

1. Tell the children that they are going to be learning about baby animals and how babies grow into adults. Ask them what the name of a baby dog is — it's a "puppy". Lots of other baby animals have special names. Ask the children to talk to a partner and write down the names of animal babies on their whiteboards. After a few minutes, take suggestions from the class, writing them down on the class whiteboard.

2. Show the children some images of baby animals on the whiteboard, and ask children whether they know which animal it is. This webpage may be useful:
animals.nationalgeographic.com/animals/photos/baby-animals
Then move onto some more unusual animals. Show pupils the baby animal, and challenge pupils to guess what type of adult animal it will grow into. You might like to use this webpage for inspiration:
www.mnn.com/earth-matters/animals/stories/8-baby-animals-that-dont-look-like-their-parents
Discuss the differences between the babies and the adults. For mammals, babies are usually just smaller — they will grow into the adult animal. In many species though, the baby looks nothing like the adult.

3. Explain the term "life cycle" to the children, pointing out that all animals have a life cycle of growth and reproduction and that some are more complicated than others.

4. Point out that mammals give birth to live young, whereas other animals lay eggs. Some animals look completely different when they first hatch!

5. Read the information on page 22 of the Activity Book together.

6. After reading, ask the children whether they think a tadpole is a different animal from a frog. It's actually a baby frog! What about a caterpillar? It's a baby butterfly or moth. Check understanding of the new words "reproduction" and "offspring". Also check that children understand that reproduction is when adults create offspring (babies can't have babies).

Phonics & Spelling Links

This lesson provides a good opportunity to teach the plurals of words ending in '-y': baby/babies; puppy/puppies; butterfly/butterflies.

Extension Questions

"Can baby animals have babies?"
Explain to children that only adult animals can reproduce and have offspring. In fact, that's what being "adult" means — it's about your body being ready to reproduce.

"Why don't we just grow forever?"
Explain to children that our bodies are programmed like a computer. There are things that they can do and things that they'll never do. So just like humans will never grow wings or be able to spin webs, we all have a maximum size. Our bodies know to stop growing when we have reached our maximum adult size. That's true for all animals, not just humans.

"Why do some animals lay eggs and others don't?"
It's mainly mammals that don't lay eggs (although a few Australian mammals do lay eggs and a few snakes have live births). So that's humans, dogs, horses, monkeys — all warm, furry things. They developed the ability to carry their tiny growing baby around with them in their bodies because it was much safer for the baby than developing in an egg. Eggs can be stolen and eaten by other animals.

7. Ask the children to complete pages 22-23 of the Activity Book. Check their understanding of the life cycles presented and address any misconceptions.

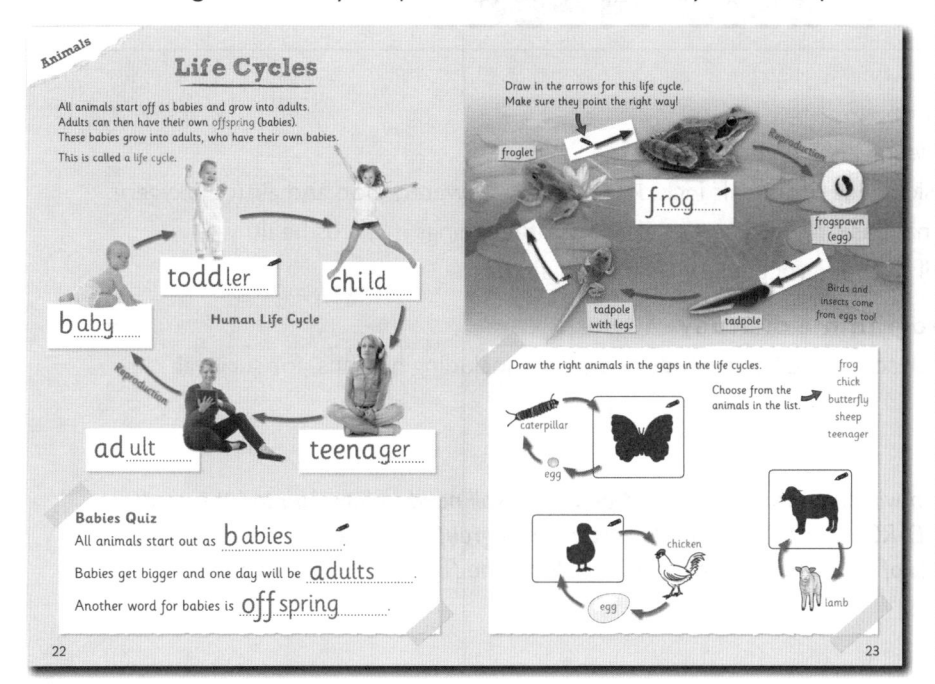

Extension Activities

Ask early finishers to draw the life cycle of a different animal of their choice. Remember to include arrows pointing in the direction of growth.

Children could also use books or the Internet to look up the life cycles of other animals. There are some unusual ones — challenge them to find the most interesting life cycle they can. Then they can share it with the rest of the class.

Plenary Questions

1. Can you name any baby animals and the adults they will turn into?

2. Can you name any baby animals that look like a different animal from their parents?

3. Can you describe the life cycle of:
   a frog?   a butterfly?   a human?   a chicken?

Follow-Up Ideas

1. Search online for life cycle videos to show the children. Look in particular for time lapse videos of a caterpillar forming a chrysalis and hatching into a butterfly, and of frogspawn turning into tadpoles and then frogs.

2. Print out the animal pictures on the CD-ROM to play a game. E.g.:

   a. Match the babies to the adults. This is a memory game where each player takes it in turn to turn over two cards. If they match, the player keeps them. If they don't match, the player turns them back over, trying to remember what they saw. The winner is the person with the most cards at the end. You will need to have printed enough cards to give one set to each pair in the class.

   b. Use pictures of different stages in a number of different animal life cycles. Give out one card each and ask the class to get into groups to show the life cycle of their animal. They then need to work out the order of their life cycle and show it to the rest of the class.

   c. Pupils could also cut out the pictures, sort them into groups and stick them into their workbooks, or onto sheets of paper. Alternatively, they could be used for a class display.

3. If your school allows it, and it's the right time of year, you can hatch your own butterflies and then release them. Buy a "Butterfly Garden" — a special net that comes with instructions, butterfly food and everything you need. You send away for the caterpillars and they arrive in the post! Watch each caterpillar make a chrysalis and then hatch into a butterfly. Alternatively, if you are lucky, you might be able to watch some frogspawn turn into tadpoles and then frogs. (Release them before they lose their tails though or you'll have tiny frogs jumping all over the classroom!) Or perhaps you could arrange for a local farm to let you borrow an incubator to hatch some chicks.

Basic Needs

Learning Objectives:
- To know the basic needs of animals including humans — water, food and air (or oxygen).
- To understand that basic needs keep us alive but other things make us healthy.
- To read and spell scientific vocabulary relating to animals.

Year 2 Science Programme of Study
"Find out about and describe the basic needs of animals, including humans, for survival (water, food and air)."

Preparation: The children will need whiteboards and pens. You will need to have printed the cards from the CD-ROM for the children to sort in small groups. You may want to provide some sheets of A3 paper and coloured pencils for the first follow-up activity.

Lesson Activities

1. Ask the children if any of them have a pet. Do they know how to look after a pet? They should talk to a partner and make a list on their whiteboards of all the things you need to do to look after a pet.

2. Take suggestions from the class about how to look after a pet. Record them on the class whiteboard if desired. Expect to see a large number of suggestions including food, water, exercise, grooming, cleaning and love.

3. Discuss all of the suggestions and add anything important which may have been missed. Ask the pupils to think about which of these are the most important. Which things would cause your pet to die if they didn't have them? Allow two minutes for children to talk to their partners before taking suggestions.

4. Explain that animals would die without food and water. They also need air to survive, but luckily we don't have to provide that! These three things are called basic needs.

5. Read page 24 of the Activity Book together.

6. Discuss the basic needs of animals, addressing any queries or misconceptions that arise. For example, children may not realise that fish can live without air — it's not really air that our bodies need, but the oxygen that's in the air. Fish get their oxygen from the water using their gills. Ensure that the children understand about the differences between animals. All animals have these three basic needs, but some can live for longer than others without air, water or food. Also, some animals can survive without shelter and some prefer to live alone.

Extension Ideas

Compare the needs of pets with the needs of zoo or farm animals and wild animals. Zoo and farm animals are kept in more natural environments and are encouraged to behave in a more natural way. Their basic needs are provided by the people who look after them. The animals should feel like they are wild but they aren't really.

Extension Questions

"Would zoo animals survive in the wild?"
If they have been allowed to behave in completely natural ways then yes. Animals like tigers that need to hunt might not be able to.

"Which animals can survive for a long time without air, food or water?"
- *Camels are adapted to live in the desert where there isn't much food or water. They store fat in their humps so they can go for months without food or water.*
- *Some whales can hold their breath for up to 90 minutes! This allows them to dive really deep searching for food.*
- *Probably the most amazing example of survival is the lungfish. The lungfish lives in water but can also breathe air when the water dries up! They bury themselves and wait for water to come back. They can live buried like this for several months without food!*

7. Ask the pupils to work through page 25 of the Activity Book:

    When they are drawing their favourite animal, it may help to have some animal names and pictures to prompt them (e.g. providing books for them to look at).

8. Compare what the children have suggested as their favourite animal's needs, noting the differences between pets and wild animals.

9. Hand out the 'Animals' Basic Needs Cards from the CD-ROM. These show images of things that pets and zoo or farm animals do and don't need. In small groups, the pupils should sort these cards into piles labelled NEED and DON'T NEED. Discuss the correct answers with the class, asking whether animals get these things in the wild. Allow a discussion among each group before answering that an animal's natural environment provides all of these things — food, water, shelter, social activity, entertainment etc. The only thing it might need that it won't get in the wild is medical attention.

Extension Ideas

Early finishers can begin to think about the needs of humans. We have the same 'basic needs' as animals, but we have 'human needs' too, like clothes and houses. This leads into a discussion on wants versus needs.

You could also ask the children to start thinking about designing a zoo. They should make sure that the animals have their basic needs covered and that they all have enough space and appropriate shelter and entertainment.

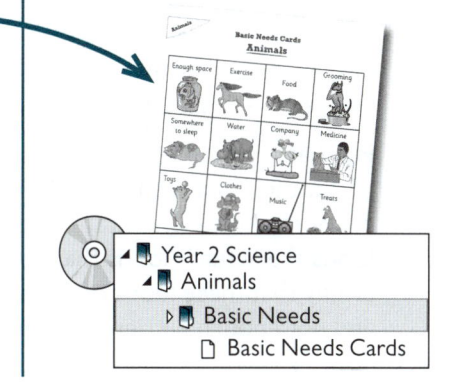

Plenary Questions

1. What are the basic needs of animals?
2. How do fish live without air?
3. How can we look after our pets properly?
4. What is the difference between a 'basic need' and something that animals need to be healthy and happy?
5. What about zoo and farm animals? Should we treat them like pets or not?

Follow-Up Ideas

1. Ask the children to design a zoo. This could lead into a great DT project or possibly an excellent homework project where each child makes a different animal's enclosure. From a list of approximately 20 different animals, children working in small groups should choose 2 or 3 animals to design an enclosure for. They should discuss what each animal needs and how their basic needs should be covered. Can any of the animals live together? Children may have seen animals such as emus and lemurs (that don't eat each other!) living together at wild animal parks that they have visited. Children should design their enclosure on paper first and then the class can talk about how to make a real 3D model of the zoo if desired. Plastic animal models would help so that the proportions are right!

2. Make sure children know the difference between WANTS and NEEDS by playing a game. Give children the 'Humans' Basic Needs Cards from the CD-ROM, making sure they understand what each item is and why you might want to have it. Then tell the children that they are going to be stranded on a desert island for a month. They can choose 10 of these items to take. What will they choose? Children should discuss this in pairs or small groups, then compare and discuss as a class. Now say they are only allowed to take 5 things. What will they take now? Children should begin to realise that they NEED certain things for survival. Discuss the difference between wants and needs.

A Balanced Diet

> **Learning Objectives:**
> - To recognise the basic food groups.
> - To identify foods which belong to each food group.
> - To understand the proportions of a balanced diet.
>
> **Year 2 Science Programme of Study**
> "Describe the importance for humans of eating the right amounts of different types of food."

Preparation: Children will need individual whiteboards and pens.
You will need paper plates, sticky labels and felt-tip pens.

Lesson Activities

1. Ask the children what their favourite meals and snacks are. Record their answers on the class whiteboard under the headings "meal" and "snack". Be careful not to ask what they had for dinner last night, or similar, as this could elicit bullying or embarrassment since the foods are going to be "judged" in this lesson.

2. Point at a few unhealthy foods from the list and ask children to put their hands up if they like this food. It will probably be most of the class. State that normally our favourite foods are actually foods that are not good for us. Explain briefly that these foods often contain too much sugar or fat and not enough nutrients that help keep us healthy.

3. Ask children to discuss with a partner what they think a healthy food is. They should make a list on their whiteboards of foods that we should eat more of. Take suggestions and discuss why they think these foods are healthy. Encourage children to think about how "natural" the foods are — the more natural and less "processed", the healthier, generally.

4. Read page 26 of the Activity Book together. Explain how the sizes of the different food segments in the circle show the proportions of these food types that we should eat. So we should have lots of fruit and veg and healthy carbohydrates, some protein and dairy (allergies/intolerances allowing), and only a small amount of fatty or sugary foods.

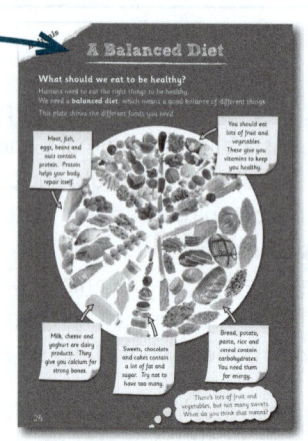

5. Ask children if they can name any foods that fit into each category. Give out some sticky labels to each small group, and ask them to write down the names of 2 or 3 different foods for each food group. If they can, they should try to come up with new foods that have not been mentioned yet and which are not shown in the Activity Book.

Phonics & Spelling Links

Use the following words to explore the different sounds of the digraph 'ea':

/iː/	eat, meat
/ɛ/	healthy, bread

Can pupils think of their own examples of 'ea' words with either of these sounds?

Teacher Notes

Be careful with misconceptions when it comes to what is "healthy". Children often think that many of their snacks are healthy, when in fact they have a very high sugar content.

Kids' yoghurts, fruity snack bars, cereal bars etc. often have a very high sugar content, and should not replace normal fruit as a healthy snack. Similarly, children's fruit drinks can have an extremely high sugar content and are still marketed as being "healthy".

Talk to the pupils about "processed" foods. Although potato waffles, for example, are mainly potato, they are not as healthy as just eating potato. When something is processed, salt, sugar and chemicals are added, and vitamins are lost. The more processed it is, the less healthy it is.

6. Draw a blank pie chart on the class whiteboard with sections to match the diagram in the Activity Book. Ask each child to come up and place a sticky label in the right part of the pie chart. Discuss each food with the class as you go, explaining why it is or is not healthy (e.g. lots of sugar/fat/protein/vitamins/calcium/energy). Leave the sticky labels on the board for future reference.

7. Ask pupils to work through page 27 of the Activity Book.

You may need to discuss some of the foods with the children to make sure they have a full understanding. For the drawing activity, they should try to make the foods the right size, so that it can be a believable meal and to encourage children to also think about portion sizes.

8. Finally, give each child a paper plate and some felt-tip pens. Ask them to draw their own version of the balanced diet plate from page 26 of the Activity Book. They should use the correct proportions, but include pictures of food that they like or eat regularly. These can then be used for a class display.

Possible Pupil Questions

"Isn't energy the same as calories? I thought calories were bad..."

Children will have heard about calories and will have a vague idea that calories, and therefore energy, is bad for you. Explain that we need energy, but it's our job to make sure we get energy in a way that gives us only energy and good things like protein or vitamins, without giving us too much fat and sugar.

"What is the fasting diet? Should I do it?"

Children will be confused between "diets" to lose weight and having a healthy diet. They should be encouraged to have a balanced diet consisting of regular healthy meals. They are growing and need plenty of energy, protein, vitamins and minerals, as well as some fats, so in no way should they be encouraged to "fast" and stop eating. Fasting might help some adults to lose weight but it is not for children, and it is easy to make yourself ill by fasting.

Plenary Questions

1. Can you describe the five different food groups?
2. Name some foods we should eat more of.
3. Name some foods we should eat less of.
4. Is this healthy or unhealthy? (List some meals and snacks.)

Follow-Up Ideas

1. Probably the best way to learn about food is to make it and eat it. Search online for children-friendly recipes to try with your class. Some recipes might be best undertaken in small groups outside of the classroom with an adult helper. Others, especially where ovens are not needed, will be easy to run as a whole class activity. Be careful to check for food allergies — you may want to send a letter home to parents, to warn them that their child will be tasting new foods, and to ask to be made aware of allergies or intolerances.

2. Children could plan a healthy three course meal for a celebrity of their choice (or perhaps link this in with another topic and plan a meal for Queen Victoria, for example). They can create menus, in the style of a cafe or restaurant, using lots of descriptive vocabulary. Make sure they are able to explain why they have chosen the different dishes on the menu and what makes them healthy.

Healthy Living

Learning Objectives:
- To understand the need for activity and exercise in daily life.
- To identify what counts as exercise and activity.
- To understand the need for hygiene.
- To identify ways in which people can be hygienic.

Year 2 Science Programme of Study
"Describe the importance for humans of exercise and hygiene."

Preparation: You will need sticky notes, A4 paper and felt-tip pens or coloured pencils. You may want a stopwatch or timer for the extension idea, and access to the Internet for early finishers.

Lesson Activities

1. Ask the class if they know what we need to do to be healthy. Hopefully they will suggest eating a balanced diet and exercising. Ask if they can name anything that counts as exercise. They are likely to name sports and gym-based activities rather than activity in general.

2. Look at the exercise photos on page 28 of the Activity Book.

3. Can they name any of these activities? Explain to the class that children their age should aim to be active for an hour every day. This can be broken up into sections, like 4 lots of 15 minutes. This activity should include something that makes them out of breath. So playing hopscotch, walking the dog, or even helping out with housework can be as good for your health as other forms of exercise, like jogging or swimming.

4. Ask the pupils to talk to their partners and write down on a sticky note something that they could do at home or in the playground that would count as exercise. Take suggestions from children, sticking their notes on the board, and discuss which of the suggestions would leave you the most out of breath.

5. Now explain to the class that being healthy is not just about diet and exercise. We can avoid getting ill through good hygiene. Ask the children if they know what hygiene means. Take suggestions and discuss their knowledge.

6. Look at the photos of good hygiene on page 28 of the Activity Book.

7. Ask the children to describe what they can see in each photo. For each activity, discuss why it helps you to stay healthy. In most cases, cleanliness stops germs from spreading to other people, so illnesses like colds and flu will not spread so easily. Apart from these things, it's also nice for other people if we don't smell horrible!

Extension Ideas

Expand a little on why exercise is good for your health. Explain that the heart pumps blood around the body and it needs to be kept strong. Like any muscle, you can make it stronger by using it more. So by doing exercise we make our hearts work and give them exercise to do. Demonstrate by having children feel their pulse or their heartbeat at rest. If possible, record the pulse (beats per minute) of a volunteer. Then have the whole class exercise for a few minutes to raise their heart rate (star jumps, running on the spot etc). They should then feel their pulse or heartbeat again. This will demonstrate to children what exercise does to the heart, reinforce the level of activity needed to have an effect and help them to understand that it will make them stronger and healthier.

Extension Activity

Ask children to rate the activities discussed in order — most strenuous (increases heart rate the most) to least strenuous.

Extension Ideas

Discuss how animals also need exercise and good hygiene to be healthy. If the pupils have any pets, they should make sure they can provide these things. For example, taking the dog for a walk and giving it a bath regularly.

8. Ask for further suggestions of things that we can do to take care of ourselves, such as going to bed early, limiting 'screen time' etc.
9. Tell the pupils to work through page 29 of the Activity Book.

Phonics & Spelling Links

Use the following words when teaching double consonants: running, jogging, swimming.

Extension Activity

Ask early finishers to use books or the Internet to find out more about germs. Typing 'germs for kids' into a search engine provides a good list of child-friendly websites. Challenge the more able pupils to find out about bacteria, viruses and fungi.

Compare and discuss children's ideas, asking them how they are going to make sure that they do these things daily.

10. Now make a class list of things that we will try to do every day to stay fit and healthy. Divide the list up so that each child has a different topic, and ask each child to make a poster to persuade people to do their thing, e.g. 'Have you just used the toilet? Now wash your hands! If you don't, you are spreading toilet germs everywhere you touch!' with an appropriate picture. Make a class display and put up certain posters around school, such as in the toilets, if appropriate.

Plenary Questions

1. Name some examples of exercise or activity.
2. How can you tell if you're doing exercise or activity that is really good for your health?
3. What might happen to you if you don't exercise?
4. What does hygiene mean? Give some examples of good hygiene.
5. Why is it important to have good hygiene?

Follow-Up Ideas

1. A good way to learn about exercise is through PE. Spend a full lesson exercising to gradually increasing intensities, using a variety of aerobic activities, stopping children and asking them to reflect on their breathing, heart rate and sweatiness. Ask children how they feel at the end. Apart from 'tired', try to elicit the response that they feel 'happy' or 'energised'.

2. Use a PE session to introduce children to activities that will raise their heart rate, and therefore count as exercise, but which are also fun. Hopefully children will remember these activities and play them themselves in the playground. Any examples of active childhood games will work well.

3. To demonstrate good hygiene practices (i.e. how to wash your hands properly), create a horrible mixture of sunflower oil, poster paint and flour. Choose a small number of children to come and coat their hands in the mixture. (The whole class can do it if you don't mind the mess!) Some should wash with cold water, some with hot water and some with hot water and soap. Now compare the results. Hopefully the children who washed with hot water and soap will have the cleanest hands, or will have found it easiest to clean them. Remind children that germs are invisible, so unless you wash with warm water and soap you are probably not washing off the germs.

The Doctor and the Vet

*'The Doctor and the Vet' is a **synoptic topic** for the Animals section. It builds on the concepts introduced in the preceding sessions and applies them to a real-world context.*

Learning Objectives:
- To understand the role of doctors and know when it is appropriate to visit a doctor.
- To identify healthy and unhealthy foods.
- To recognise the outcomes of an unhealthy lifestyle and suggest healthier alternatives.
- To understand that owners have a responsibility to provide for the needs of their pet.
- To recognise examples of reproduction in animals other than humans.

Year 2 Science Programme of Study
"Notice that animals, including humans, have offspring which grow into adults. Find out about and describe the basic needs of animals, including humans, for survival (water, food and air). Describe the importance for humans of exercise, eating the right amounts of different types of food, and hygiene."

Preparation: Children will need coloured crayons. You will need to print the cards from the CD-ROM for the second part of this lesson. You may want to provide children with vet and doctor role-play costumes and props.

Lesson Activities

1. Ask children to put their hand up if they have ever been to the doctor (GP). Ask them to put their hand up if they've ever taken an animal to the vet. What do doctors and vets do? Write children's suggestions on the class whiteboard. Make sure that children understand the full range of doctors' and vets' work, e.g. prescribing medicine, referring you to the hospital for tests or surgery, giving out health advice, visiting you at home, dealing with emergencies.

2. Discuss with children when it is appropriate to go to the doctor and when it is not. Explain that if doctors are dealing with minor things, then people who are really ill might have to wait. But if it's an emergency, get treatment as soon as you can. Ask children to talk to a partner about what you should go to A+E about, or to a GP, and what you can treat at home. Take suggestions, making a list on the board under three headings — 'Go to A+E or call 999', 'Go to your GP' and 'Treat it yourself'.

3. Look at page 30 of the Activity Book. Explain that doctors give out a lot of health advice. What types of foods might the first doctor and patient be talking about? Model an example answer. What might the second doctor be saying? Take suggestions and discuss the importance of a balanced diet (i.e. it's OK to have a small amount of sugar or fat in moderation along with lots of healthy foods).

4. Remind children about the term 'basic needs'. Can they remember what animals' basic needs are and what else they need to be happy and healthy?

Phonics & Spelling Links

*In this section pupils have come across lots of words with 'c' followed by 'e', 'i' or 'y', making an /s/ sound: 'cal**c**ium', '**c**ycle', '**c**ereal', 'exer**c**ise', 'dan**c**e'. Challenge your more able spellers to learn the spellings of these words.*

Teacher Notes

If you are unsure about what counts as an illness that you should see a doctor about, have a look at the NHS website. Tell children that when you aren't sure whether you should go to the doctor, parents can call the non-emergency number (111) for advice. Obviously, call 999 in a life-threatening emergency.

Ideas for 'Go to A+E' — broken bone, serious bleeding, stopped breathing, severe allergic reaction.

Ideas for 'Go to your GP' — something that hasn't cleared up after ten days, infections, things that need checking like unusual moles.

Ideas for 'Treat it yourself' — minor cuts and bruises, sunburn, insect bites and stings, coughs and colds, spots and rashes, sickness and diarrhoea.

5. Now look at page 31 of the Activity Book. Take suggestions about what we need to provide to look after a dog. Look at the second example — why has the bird laid eggs? What will happen to them? Work with children to model an example answer.

6. Once you've discussed the scenarios as a class, the pupils should independently complete the Activity Book pages. They could write the responses in words or draw pictures to represent what is being said.

7. When they have finished, tell the pupils that they are going to be carrying out a role-playing activity. The pupils should find a partner and take a card (print these from the CD-ROM). The cards provide vet- and doctor-patient role-play scenarios for children to prepare. If possible, provide appropriate role-play costumes and props. Encourage children to make their role-play believable and to act with expression and eye-contact — e.g. they should greet each other politely, have a full discussion in a professional manner and then say goodbye politely. The cards only briefly describe the scenarios, so you should help the children to think about how the conversation would go. Take it in turns to show each role-play to the rest of the class and to discuss the scenario if there is any issue that you feel it is important to raise.

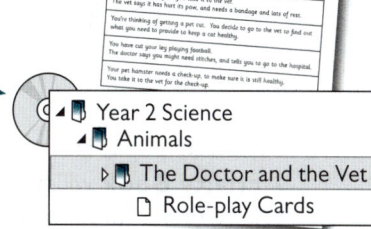

Extension Ideas

The pupils could think of their own doctor or vet scenarios to act out, in addition to those suggested.

Plenary Questions

1. What do vets and doctors do?
2. What would a doctor advise you to do if you were becoming overweight?
3. What would a doctor advise you to eat less of if you were feeling run down and becoming overweight?
4. To feel healthier, what would a doctor advise you to eat more of?
5. What do we need to do to look after our pets properly?
6. Why do birds lay eggs? What do other animals do instead?
7. Should you go to the doctor if you had...? (List examples of issues and illnesses.)

Follow-Up Ideas

1. Ask the pupils to think of as many injuries or illnesses/symptoms as they can. These should range from very minor to very severe, e.g. *grazed knee, chicken pox, broken arm, stopped breathing*. These can then be written down on cards to play a sorting game. The children can work in small groups to sort the cards into piles of 'Go to A+E', 'Go to GP' or 'Treat yourself'. At the end, check children's understanding and address any misconceptions.

2. If possible, arrange a visit from a local GP or vet. If appropriate, ask them to bring in examples of tools they use or photos that illustrate their job. In advance, children should prepare questions to ask. Similarly, it may be possible to arrange a visit from a fitness professional or nutritionist.

3. Show children leaflets from your local GP or vet's surgery (or both). There will normally be lots of leaflets about hygiene, not spreading germs, how to stay healthy in general, recognising symptoms of certain illnesses, caring for others etc. Children should use these leaflets as inspiration to create their own advice leaflet, for either a vet or doctor to give out.

Notes on Assessment (Animals)

You'll need to assess pupils' understanding of both the knowledge-based requirements from the Science Programme of Study and the 'Working Scientifically' requirements that underpin the Key Stage 1 curriculum.

> The 'Animals' section gives opportunities for pupils to **work scientifically** by:
> - Performing simple tests.
> - Identifying and classifying.
> - Gathering and recording data to help in answering questions.

The tasks pupils complete in the **Activity Book** will help you assess pupils' understanding of the 'Animals, including humans' section of the Year 2 Programme of Study.

For both the 'Animals, including humans' section of the Programme of Study and the 'Working Scientifically' requirements, you can use **Classroom Assessment**.

This will allow pupils who may not have strong literacy skills to demonstrate their understanding practically and verbally.

Year 2 Science Programme of Study: ANIMALS, INCLUDING HUMANS				KS1 Science: Working Scientifically		
Notice that animals, including humans, have offspring which grow into adults	Find out about and describe the basic needs of animals, including humans, for survival (water, food and air)	Describe the importance for humans of exercise, eating the right amounts of different types of food, and hygiene		Performing simple tests	Identifying and classifying	Gathering and recording data to help in answering questions

Classroom Assessment

Classroom Assessment should be in the form of small-group work, observation and the use of open-ended questions. Try focusing on just five or six pupils in each lesson, so you get a deeper understanding of the level they're working at.

Session 1: Life Cycles

In this lesson pupils learn about how baby animals grow into adults. You can use this as a springboard for children to begin to identify and classify animals, by pointing out their similarities and differences. Some pupils may also be able to classify animals using groupings such as mammals, amphibians etc. Work with a mixed ability group and notice who is starting to do this, using the information from the lesson.

Prompt Questions

Can anyone name two animals that are the same in some way? How are they the same? How are they different? Which animals grow just grow bigger and which change their shape completely? What sorts of animals tend to change most? Why might this be?

84   Year 2: Section Three — Animals

Session 2: Basic Needs

During this lesson children will continue to build on their classification skills, while also learning to identify more common animals. Work with a mixed ability group (or share your time between two or three), while children complete the Basic Needs Cards activity from the CD-ROM. Which pupils demonstrate a good knowledge of what humans and animals need to survive? Who is able to use this information to sort the items into groups, giving reasons for their groupings?

Prompt Questions
Tell me about how you've sorted your cards. Why do you think animals need these things to survive? Were there any cards you found tricky to place? Tell me about those.

Session 3: A Balanced Diet

Continue to work with mixed ability groups to assess pupils' knowledge against the learning objectives, as well as their ability to identify and classify, this time into healthy and unhealthy food groups. You could also use part of this lesson to target pupils who did not meet lesson objectives from the previous lessons and to do some small group/intervention work.

Prompt Questions
Tell me about the foods you have chosen for your plates. Which ones are the healthiest? Are there any that are less healthy? Tell me why you think that. Can you think of any foods that are hard to classify? Why is that?

Session 4: Healthy Living

Use the first or second Follow-Up Ideas to give children the chance to carry out a simple test in order to answer the question, 'Which activity raises my heart rate the most?' Children can work in pairs or small groups with a stopwatch to count how many times their heart beats in a minute after a series of different actions.

Prompt Questions
Tell me about your experiment. What data have you collected? What does that tell you? Which activity raised your heart rate the most/least? Why do you think that is? If we did the test again would you do anything differently?

Session 5: The Doctor and the Vet

Children will be working in mixed ability pairs to create a role play, providing you with a good opportunity to assess the class's knowledge, focusing in particular on any children whose progress you are not sure about. Observe as they prepare their role plays. Who includes information from previous lessons? Who is able to make their scenario believable by using sound knowledge about animals and their needs?

Intervention
You might like to choose a few lower-ability pupils to work with as a small group. Focus on the knowledge-based objectives from the Programme of Study and note down anything they say that demonstrates good understanding.

Recording Pupils' Attainment

By the end of the topic, you should be confident in your judgement of which pupils in your class have met the topic's learning objectives. You should also know which pupils are yet to meet the learning objectives and which children have moved beyond the Year Two Programme of Study with additional skills and knowledge.

Record pupils' attainment in the Assessment Grid on the CD-ROM. You may wish to use a traffic light system to colour-code the grid.

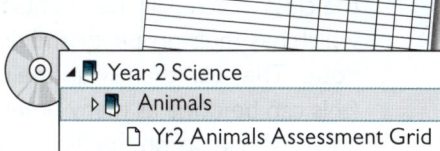

Year 2: Section Three — Animals

Year 2: Section Four — Materials
Which Material Should I Use?

> **Learning Objectives:**
> - To recap everyday materials from Year 1.
> - To link the properties of a material to its purpose/uses.
>
> **Year 2 Science Programme of Study**
> "Identify and compare the suitability of a variety of everyday materials, including wood, metal, plastic, glass, brick, rock, paper and cardboard for particular uses."

Preparation: *Prepare a flipchart, pens and sticky notes.*

Ensure that there are plenty of objects in the classroom (or elsewhere in the school) for the children to find a variety of materials (see those listed in the PoS above) and properties (hard, soft, rough, smooth, shiny, dull, rigid, flexible, transparent, opaque, strong, brittle, waterproof, absorbent, lightweight, heavy). Place extra items around the room if necessary.

Provide the children with spoons made from different materials — wood, metal, plastic.

Lesson Activities

1. Write the word 'material' on the flipchart and ask the children to tell you what it means. (This should be a recap from Year 1.) Reinforce the fact that we use this word in science as a general word for what an object is made from, rather than as another word for 'fabric' (as is often used in everyday language).

2. Ask the children to look for objects around the classroom (you could also send pupils to look in different places around the school) and discuss with a partner what materials the objects are made from, writing their ideas on sticky notes.

3. Take feedback from the pupils and stick all of the different materials on the flipchart sheet. (In addition to the materials listed in the Programme of Study, they may find materials such as leather, rubber, clay and fabric.)

4. Can anyone find any similar objects that are made from different materials — for example, a metal pencil sharpener and a plastic one? Ask them to discuss the good and bad points of making this type of object from different materials — for example, plastic sharpeners are cheaper to buy and can be made in different colours, but metal sharpeners tend to last longer.

5. Write the word 'properties' on a new flipchart sheet and ask the children if they know what it means. (Again this should be a recap from Year 1.) Discuss the fact that the properties of a material tell us what it is like and how it behaves. Can they give you some examples of properties? Record these on the flipchart.

6. Ask each pair to choose a property and write it on a sticky note, ensuring that there is a good range of properties across the class. Each pair then hunts for an object in the classroom which has their property and draws/writes it on their sticky note. They can then swap their property with another group (this can be done as many times as you decide) and you can collect the ideas on the flipchart.

Extension Activity

Give the children spoons made from wood, metal and plastic to investigate. Ask for their ideas about why the spoons are made from these materials (e.g. they don't bend, they can be cleaned easily). They can discuss the different uses of the spoons depending on the materials they are made from. For example, metal spoons for everyday use (hardwearing), plastic spoons for picnics (cheap and disposable), wooden spoons for cooking (they don't scratch the bases of pans).

Would materials such as glass, paper, cardboard or fabric be suitable to make spoons? Ask the children to explain why not (e.g. a fabric spoon would be too flexible/soft, a glass spoon might break, a paper/cardboard spoon would not be waterproof).

7. Discuss the materials that the objects are made from and how the properties of these materials make them suitable for that purpose. For example, "the cushion cover is made of fabric because it is soft and flexible". They may find objects made from more than one material — for example "the chair is made from plastic and metal because these materials are strong and rigid".

8. Ask the pupils to read page 32 and work through page 33 of the Activity Book. Some of the sentences could have more than one answer. Talk to the children about their answers to ensure that they can justify their choices.

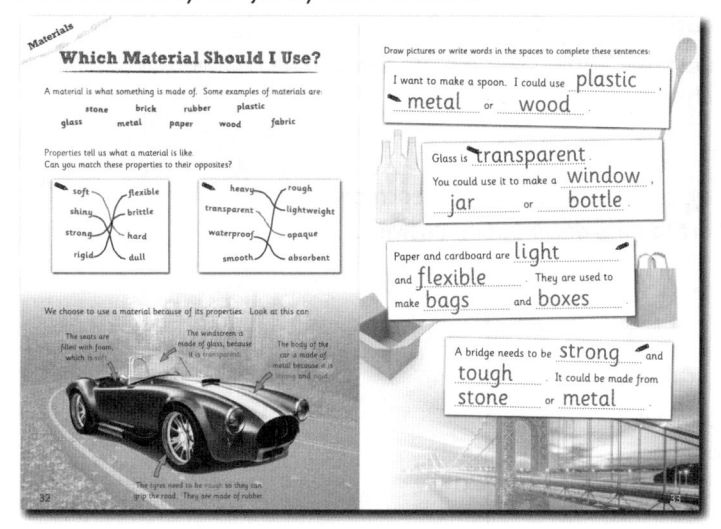

Extension Ideas

Pupils could draw a picture of something else that is made of many different materials, for example a computer or a building, and label the materials with their properties.

Extension Activity

The following activity can be carried out with the children to reinforce the properties of different materials and their suitability for making particular products:
www.bbc.co.uk/schools/scienceclips/ages/7_8/ characteristics_materials.shtml

In the 'testing room', they can carry out a virtual experiment into whether glass, metal, paper, plastic, fabric and rubber are flexible, strong, transparent or waterproof. In the 'workshop', they can try using different materials to make particular objects, including a car tyre and a sports bottle, with an explanation/illustration of how each material would behave.

Plenary Questions

1. What does the word 'material' mean? Can you name 5 different materials?

2. What are 'properties'? Can you name 5 properties of materials?

3. Explain why windows are usually made of glass.

4. Give two different materials that could be used to make a ruler and explain why the properties of these materials would make them suitable.

Follow-Up Ideas

1. Using the worksheet from the CD-ROM, carry out simple experiments to test the properties of different materials. Ask the children to help you decide how you can test the different properties in a scientific way. E.g. for absorbency: fill a measuring jug with water and record the level of the water. Place the material into the water, leave it for a few seconds, then remove. Now measure the water level again to see how much has been absorbed by the material. Also introduce the idea of a fair test. (Take extra care when testing glass.)

    - Year 2 Science
      - Materials
        - Which Material Should I Use
        - Testing Properties

2. Investigate how materials used for building houses have changed. For example, the children could research materials used in Tudor times for building houses — wooden beams, wattle and daub walls, wooden shutters or single pane glass windows, thatched roof, straw on the floor, wooden bucket for a toilet — and compare with the materials used for building modern houses. They could be given pictures to label, draw or paint their own pictures or make models.

3. Go on a class walk to look for different materials in your local area. This could include natural and man-made materials. Look at the materials used in your school building (inside and outside) and discuss why they might have been chosen.

4. Look at the different materials used for clothing, e.g. waterproof coats, fluorescent jackets, warm wool or fleece items. Again, this could be linked to history as a comparison of how clothing materials have changed over time.

Changing Materials

Learning Objectives:
- To understand how new objects can be made by changing the shapes of materials in different ways.
- To experiment with changing modelling clay by squashing, bending, twisting and stretching it into different shapes.

Year 2 Science Programme of Study
"Find out how the shapes of solid objects made from some materials can be changed by squashing, bending, twisting and stretching."

Preparation: Provide a ball of modelling clay, such as Plasticine®, for each child. You may wish to use a flipchart to note down pupils' answers.

Lesson Activities

1. Provide each child with a ball of modelling clay. Allow some time for them to play with it and explore its properties. Ask them to describe its properties, encouraging them to use words from the previous session (flexible, soft etc.).

2. Demonstrate to the class how you can make something out of a ball of modelling clay. Ask them questions about what you are doing to change the shape of the original ball — rolling, twisting, stretching, pulling, squashing, bending, flattening, pinching etc. Write these words on a whiteboard/flipchart.

3. Now ask each child to make something with their own modelling clay — this could be a free choice, or you may want them to make something specific, such as their favourite animal or a person. Ask them to describe to their partners how they made their object from their ball of modelling clay, encouraging them to use the words you recorded. Add any new words they use to your list.

4. Read page 34 of the Activity Book together and discuss how the materials were changed to make the various objects.

Extension Ideas

You may choose to introduce some more complex vocabulary, for example 'pliable' (capable of being bent or shaped), 'adaptable' (able to be modified for different purposes) or 'malleable' (can be pressed into a shape without breaking).

Extension Ideas

If the children have made models of animals or people, they could get together in groups to create simple stop motion animations. There is some free software here which may be helpful:

www.ticklypictures.com/projects/jellycam

This video also offers a good introduction:

www.bbc.co.uk/programmes/p013bhgy

Phonics & Spelling Links

Verbs like *stretch*, *squash* and *twist* contain lots of consonant clusters. Explore the sounds of these words in relation to their meaning — do they sound like the action they describe in some way?

5. Ask the children to work through page 35 of the Activity Book:

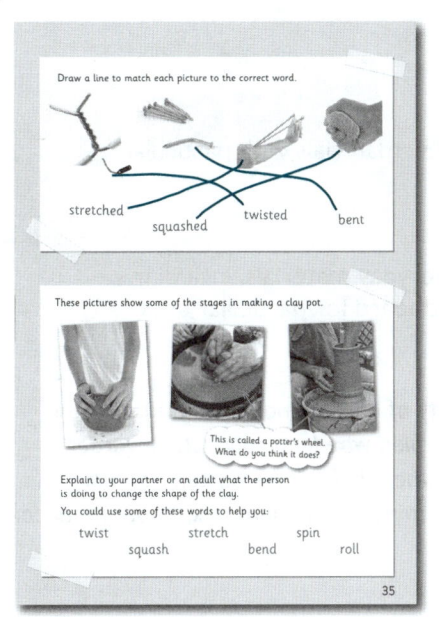

6. Talk about how easy or difficult it is to change some materials back again. Compare the clay pot in the Activity Book with the objects they made earlier in the session. Clay usually goes hard (after a while being left in the air or when heated in an oven/kiln), whereas Plasticine® remains flexible.

7. How do they think this might affect the uses of the two types of material? For example, Plasticine® is ideal for making temporary models (such as those used in stop motion animation or for playing), while clay is better for creating more permanent objects (such as cups, bowls, tiles or statues).

Teacher Notes

You may want to find a video online of a clay pot being made. You can show this to the class to help them describe how the shape of the clay is changed.

Extension Activity

The children could make their own bowls, tiles or sculptures from air-drying clay. They could experiment with using different 'tools' to decorate them — for example, pressing natural items like shells or leaves into the damp clay to leave an imprint. They could then paint them when fully dry.

Extension Ideas

Pupils could think about other ways in which materials can be changed. For example, a change in temperature often results in a change in a material's properties:

- What happens to chocolate when you heat it?
- What happens to water when you make it really cold (e.g. by putting it in the freezer)?
- Did you know that heating sand to a very high temperature lets you shape it into glass?

Would these materials change back to how they were if the temperature went back to normal?

Plenary Questions

1. How can we change materials? Think of four words to describe what you could do to change the shape of a piece of modelling clay.

2. Explain how you could change a straight piece of wire into something new.

3. Why do we need to change materials?

Follow-Up Ideas

1. The children (working in groups of 3 or 4) could make their own playdough, using the instructions on the CD-ROM). Encourage them to discuss the properties of the ingredients as they mix them and talk about the changes that take place.

2. Make some 'slime'. You can use the instructions here: www.sublimescience.com/free-science-experiments/how-to-make-slime
Talk about the different properties that the slime has — it's hard when you prod it quickly, but if you pour it over your hands it feels runny!
Ask the children to come up with some ideas for possible uses of their slime.

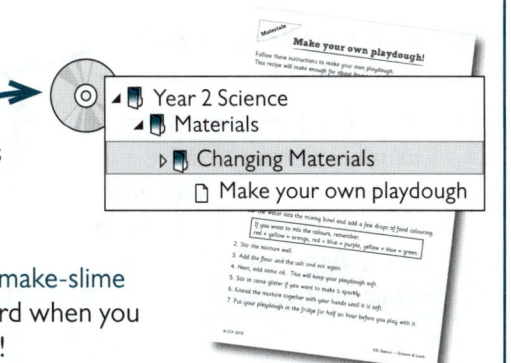

Inventors Gallery

> **Learning Objectives:**
> - To identify natural and man-made materials.
> - To learn about some people who have created new materials with particular properties.
>
> **Year 2 Science Programme of Study**
> "Identify and compare the suitability of a variety of everyday materials, including wood, metal, plastic, glass, brick, rock, paper and cardboard for particular uses."

Preparation: Provide two large PE hoops, as well as a variety of objects made from natural and man-made materials (e.g. natural — wooden ruler, wooden spoon, stone garden ornament, wool scarf, cotton handkerchief, leather shoe, slate coaster, iron nail; man-made — plastic bottle, plastic bag, glass mirror, cardboard box, paper notebook.)

Lesson Activities

1. Recap the words '*materials*' and '*properties*' and ask the children to explain their meanings, based on their prior learning.

2. Ask the children to give you examples of how properties of certain materials make them suitable for particular uses, encouraging them to use vocabulary from previous sessions.

3. Hand out objects made from natural and man-made materials (see the suggestions above) and ask the children to decide which category they fit into. (Ensure that they are focusing on the materials rather than the objects — all of the objects have been manufactured, but they are thinking about the main materials used to make the objects.) You could use two large PE hoops for sorting the objects.

4. Explain that natural materials come from plants, animals or rocks (e.g. cotton, wood, leather, wool, stone, metals), and that man-made materials are created by changing natural materials (e.g. glass is made from sand, plastic comes from oil, paper and cardboard are made from wood). Discuss the fact that humans have found ways of improving or adapting natural materials to make them suitable for different uses.

5. Read page 36 of the Activity Book together.

6. Talk about how new things are usually invented to solve a problem. Can they tell you what problems the inventions in the Activity Book were designed to solve?

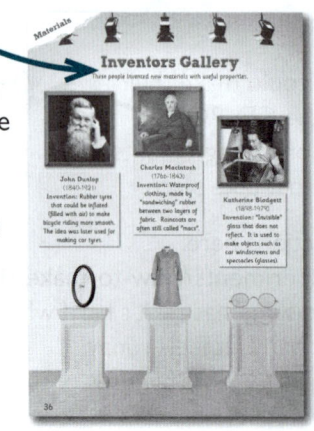

Extension Ideas

- *Show photographs of plants that give us natural materials. Good places to search for these are on the websites of botanical gardens, for example: www.edenproject.com or www.kew.org*
- *Show the children a video of glass blowing to demonstrate a traditional method of making glass. For example: www.bbc.co.uk/education/clips/zh4g9j6*

Teacher Notes

Pupils may be interested to know more about how we get some common materials from plants:

Cotton — *when the flowers of the cotton plant (Gossypium hirsutum) wither, the seed pods (called bolls) produce fluffy lumps of cotton, which is collected and then spun to produce cotton fibres and threads.*

Sisal — *the leaves of the Agave sisalana plant contain threads that are used to make sisal; this is a coarse string used in items such as carpets, or some children may recognise it as being used on cat scratching posts.*

Rubber — *cuts are made in the bark of the rubber tree (Hevea brasiliensis) and liquid latex is collected to produce rubber (this is called 'tapping'). Natural rubber has some uses but it is more useful after undergoing a chemical process called vulcanisation.*

7. Ask the children to work through page 37 of the Activity Book.

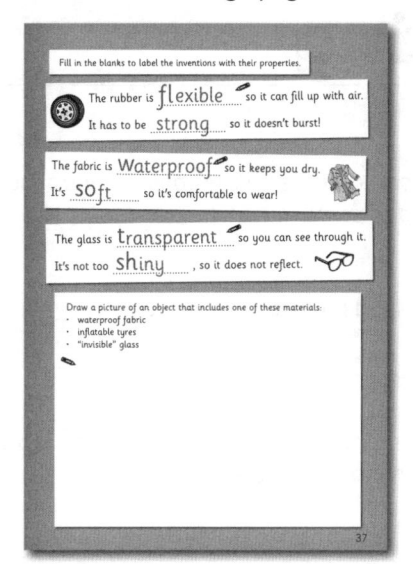

8. Now ask the children to design their own inventions to solve particular problems. For example — a bedroom-tidying machine, a healthy sauce that makes all foods taste like chocolate, rocket shoes to get them home from school quicker! Begin by asking them to tell you some things that frustrate them in everyday life and record these on a flipchart/whiteboard. In groups, ask them to choose a 'problem' (or you might decide to allocate one to each group) and to work together to design an invention to solve this problem. They can use any materials they like, as they will just be designing their invention and not actually making it. They can use copies of the 'Be an Inventor!' sheet to record their ideas. There are also some invention ideas on this website that you could share with the children:
www.inventions-handbook.com/invention-ideas-for-kids.html

9. The groups could pitch their invention ideas to a panel (perhaps made up of children from another class or senior staff from your school) in a "Dragon's Den" style session. You could watch this video together for some examples of pitches from children: www.youtube.com/watch?v=H0kbMpQ5Qc4

Extension Ideas

Tell the children about some other inventors, or ask them to do their own research. For example:

John McAdam (1756-1836) — a Scottish engineer who developed a new system of building roads to make them curved. These have a surface made up of lots of small stones laid tightly together, allowing water to run to the sides. The material tarmac is based on his invention and is named after him. You could take the children outside to look at the surface of the pavements/roads near your school.

Bette Nesmith Graham (1924-1980) — an American secretary who invented a correction fluid called "Mistake Out". This was 'liquid paper' that could be used to cover up mistakes and then dried so that you could write (or type, in her case) over it. You could show the children a bottle of modern correction fluid and explain how it works.

Elif Bilgin — a Turkish teenager who made a new type of plastic using banana peel. She wanted to see if plastic could be made from waste materials rather than extracting more oil from under the ground. She made her discovery at the age of just 16! There is a video of her story and other information on her website: www.elif-bilgin.com

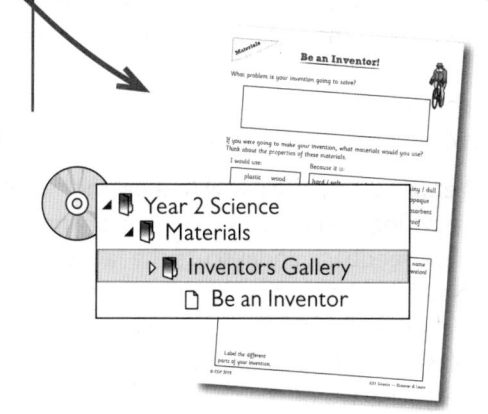

Plenary Questions

1. Why do humans sometimes need to change natural materials?
2. Tell me about someone who invented a new material.
3. If you could invent something, what would it be? What materials would you use? Why?

Follow-Up Ideas

1. Look at some more inventions that have been designed to solve problems, for example the "ballbarrow", designed by James Dyson in 1974 because he was frustrated when the narrow wheel of his wheelbarrow kept getting stuck in the mud. You could also look at items invented by children, such as ear-muffs and the trampoline: www.greatbusinessschools.org/10-great-inventions-dreamt-up-by-children

2. Show the children some rather more silly inventions (gadgets), such as the baby mop onesie, spinning spaghetti fork or the umbrella with a cup holder — all of which are available to buy online!

Recycling

'Recycling' is a **synoptic topic** for the Materials section. It builds on the concepts introduced in the preceding sessions and applies them to a real-world context.

Learning Objectives:
- To understand that waste materials can be changed into new products.
- To think of new uses for everyday materials.

Year 2 Science Programme of Study
"Identify and compare the suitability of a variety of everyday materials, including wood, metal, plastic, glass, brick, rock, paper and cardboard for particular uses."

Preparation: You will need:

The recycling symbol, which you can find on the CD-ROM.

A bag of clean, mixed rubbish for sorting (e.g. plastic bottles, newspaper, glass jars with metal lids, drinks cans; no food waste or anything sharp).

Plastic bottles of various types and sizes, including plastic milk bottles (you could ask each child to bring one in) — ensure that they are thoroughly washed.

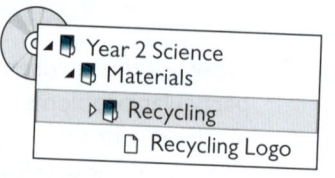

- Year 2 Science
  - Materials
    - Recycling
      - Recycling Logo

Lesson Activities

1. Show the children a recycling symbol (without telling them what it is) and discuss the shape — arrows going round in the same direction. What might this mean? Ask if anyone has seen this logo before and what they think it represents. Do any of the children recycle at home? Can they tell you any materials that can be recycled? Ask them to help you sort a bag of rubbish into different materials and talk about which ones can be recycled.

2. Let the pupils discuss with a partner why we should bother recycling, rather than simply throwing everything away. Take feedback and discuss the fact that materials such as plastic and glass take a very long time to decompose (rot or break down). Recap from the previous session how plastic, paper and glass are made from natural materials, so recycling avoids the need to cut down more trees or extract more oil. You could also talk about the impact of our rubbish on wildlife (e.g. animals getting trapped in plastic bottles, sea creatures eating plastic bags, foxes scavenging in metal food tins and getting cut).

3. Read pages 38 and 39 of the Activity Book together and ask the children to complete the activities.

Extension Ideas

You could also talk about composting food waste and explain that items such as fruit, leaves and egg shells decompose easily — unlike materials such as plastic or glass — and this adds extra nutrients to the soil. If you have a compost bin/heap at school, or there is one at a local allotment that you can visit, allow the children to look at and smell it. They may also be able to feel the heat generated by the waste being broken down.

Show the children a photograph of a landfill site. Ask them to imagine what it looks, smells and sounds like there. Would they like to live near a landfill site? Explain that we will run out of space for new landfill sites if we do not find other ways of dealing with our waste, such as recycling.

You could even make your own landfill. Put a thick layer of soil into the bottom of a bucket or similar container. Add a layer of rubbish items on top of the soil, including some food waste (e.g. apple cores, banana peel, carrot tops, tea bags). Ask the children to predict which objects will rot. Cover the rubbish with another layer of soil and sprinkle with water. Repeat the steps with more rubbish items. Mix up the contents using a spoon or spade twice a week and add water to keep it moist. After a few weeks, empty the contents onto newspaper and inspect the materials that are left.

4. Explain to the class how, as well as industrial recycling where our rubbish is taken away to be turned into something new, we can also try our own version of recycling at home. Taking old items that we've used and then turning them into something fun or useful is much better than just throwing them away. We can recycle pretty much anything this way — we just need to use our imagination!

5. Hand out some plastic bottles. Each child (or pair) can use their plastic bottle to make something new. Here are some simple ideas to help them (some aspects will need adult support):

    - Watering can: poke holes in the lid of a plastic milk bottle, decorate with waterproof paint or permanent marker pens and fill with water.

    - Bird feeder: cut a hole in a plastic drinks bottle (big enough for birds to feed from but not so big that the seeds/nuts fall out). Add two smaller holes either side to poke through an old pencil or piece of dowel for a bird to perch on. Tie string tightly around the neck for hanging the feeder.

    - Pencil pot: cut off the top half of a bottle, wrap coloured paper round the bottom half and decorate. (Old jars or juice cartons can also be used for this purpose.)

    - Musical instrument: fill with dry beans to make a shaker. You can poke long nails into the sides of the bottle to make it into a rainmaker, as the beans catch the nails on their way down the bottle. The class could make other instruments from waste products (e.g. metal saucepan lids for cymbals, plastic boxes for drums, wooden spoons for beaters) and create a 'Rubbish Orchestra'!

    - Gardening scoop: simply cut the top half off a plastic milk bottle and then hold by the handle to scoop up soil. It can also be used for filling bird feeders by scooping up seeds and then taking off the lid to release them into the feeder.

Teacher Notes

The Science section of the website www.recycling-guide.org.uk shows pictures of the steps of recycling paper, glass and aluminium, which could be shared with the children.

Extension Ideas

Explain that the metal containers we recycle are usually made of either aluminium or steel. These are separated at the recycling plant, so that the different metals don't get mixed up. It's easy to separate them because steel will stick to a magnet but aluminium will not. You could provide a mixture of steel and aluminium cans for the children to sort using magnets.

Teacher Notes

Pupils should try to link the objects they have made back to earlier sessions. What are the properties of the plastic bottle that make it suitable for making a particular object? How have the pupils changed the material? (Have they bent, squashed, twisted it etc?)

Extension Ideas

The pupils could try making things out of a range of different items — old jars, cardboard boxes, other types of packaging... whatever they can find!

Plenary Questions

1. What does 'recycling' mean? Why is it important to recycle?
2. Which materials can be recycled? How are they changed into new products?

Follow-Up Ideas

1. Ask the children to bring in some old socks — these might have holes in or be odd, but ensure that parental permission has been given! They can use these to make sock puppets, adding beads or buttons for eyes, felt for a tongue, card for scales etc.

2. Host a school assembly so that the children can talk about recycling and why it is important. They could use their sock puppets to present it!

3. Find uses for other waste items — for example, in the school garden you could hang up old CDs as bird scarers when seeds are planted, use old/odd wellies as planters or make plastic bottle cloches to protect plants.

4. Some recycling plants offer school visits. Contact your nearest plant or search online to see if you can organise a trip.

Notes on Assessment (Materials)

You'll need to assess pupils' understanding of both the knowledge-based requirements from the Science Programme of Study and the 'Working Scientifically' requirements that underpin the Key Stage 1 curriculum.

> The 'Materials' section gives opportunities for pupils to **work scientifically** by:
> - Observing closely, using simple equipment.
> - Performing simple tests.
> - Identifying and classifying.
> - Using their observations and ideas to suggest answers to questions.

The tasks pupils complete in the **Activity Book** will help you assess pupils' understanding of the 'Uses of Everyday Materials' section of the Year 2 Programme of Study.

Year 2 Science Programme of Study: USES OF EVERYDAY MATERIALS		KS1 Science: Working Scientifically			
Identify and compare the suitability of a variety of everyday materials, including wood, metal, plastic, glass, brick, rock, paper and cardboard for particular uses	Find out how the shapes of solid objects made from some materials can be changed by squashing, bending, twisting and stretching	Observing closely, using simple equipment	Performing simple tests	Identifying and classifying	Using their observations and ideas to suggest answers to questions

For both the 'Uses of Everyday Materials' section of the Programme of Study and the 'Working Scientifically' requirements, you can use **Classroom Assessment**.

This will allow pupils who may not have strong literacy skills to demonstrate their understanding practically and verbally.

Classroom Assessment

Classroom Assessment should be in the form of small-group work, observation and the use of open-ended questions. Try focusing on just five or six pupils in each lesson, so you get a deeper understanding of the level they're working at.

Session 1: Which Material Should I Use?

Use the worksheet on the CD-ROM (see the first Follow-Up Idea), to plan and carry out a simple test. Choose some of your more able scientists and encourage them to think of different ways to test different properties in a range of materials. Which pupils can come up with workable suggestions? Who is beginning to make a link between collecting data and answering a question such as, 'Which material is most absorbent?'

Prompt Questions
How could we find out which material is the most flexible / hardest / most transparent? What information would we need to collect? What would we need to keep the same each time? What do you predict we will find out? Can you explain your answer?

Y2 Science PoS: Materials		Working Scientifically			
Identify and compare the suitability of a variety of everyday materials, including wood, metal, plastic, glass, brick, rock, paper and cardboard for particular uses	Find out how the shapes of solid objects made from some materials can be changed by squashing, bending, twisting and stretching	Observing closely, using simple equipment	Performing simple tests	Identifying and classifying	Using their observations and ideas to suggest answers to questions
✓		✓	✓	✓	✓

Session 2: Changing Materials

In this lesson children will change the shape of Plasticine® using different actions. Sit and work with a mixed ability group and use questioning to encourage them to closely observe what is happening to their material, thinking about and noting down any good words which describe either what they are doing or what is happening to the Plasticine®.

Prompt Questions
Tell me what you are doing. What is happening to the Plasticine® when you do that? Could you change the shape of the table in the same way? Why not? How are they different? What properties does Plasticine® have that makes it easy to change its shape?

Session 3: Inventors Gallery

In this lesson you are assessing which children can use their observations of materials and their properties to design their own inventions. Try to spend a little time with each group and observe their discussions and decision-making processes. Remind them it is not enough to just invent a product, they also have to be able to justify the use of each material they have used.

Intervention
This would be a good lesson to spend some time with any pupils who have not met the knowledge objectives from this unit. Use the design activity to talk about everyday materials, their properties and how they can be used to make things.

Session 4: Recycling

Use the whole-class section of this lesson to focus on your less able scientists. Give them support to identify the different materials in the rubbish bag and classify them into those that can be recycled and those that cannot. Later in the lesson you might like to talk to a few mixed ability pairs and ask them to sort the materials in other ways in order to demonstrate their ability to classify.

Prompt Questions
Who can tell me what this is made from? Tell me about that material. Do you think it can be recycled or not? Can you see any other materials that can be recycled? Are there any materials that you're not sure about?

Recording Pupils' Attainment

By the end of the topic, you should be confident in your judgement of which pupils in your class have met the topic's learning objectives. You should also know which pupils are yet to meet the learning objectives and which children have moved beyond the Year Two Programme of Study with additional skills and knowledge.

Record pupils' attainment in the Assessment Grid on the CD-ROM. You may wish to use a traffic light system to colour-code the grid.

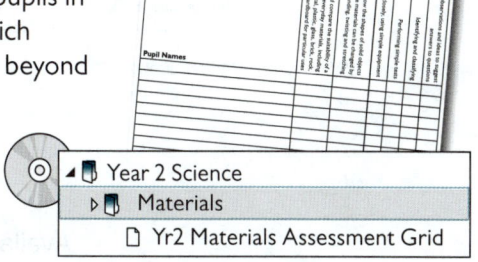

▲ 🗐 Year 2 Science
  ▷ 🗐 Materials
      🗋 Yr2 Materials Assessment Grid

Year 2: Section Four — Materials

Also available in CGP's range for ages 5-7...

KS1 SATS — Unbeatable SATS preparation for Maths and English

KS1 Maths — Clear study notes and plenty of practice for every topic

KS1 English — Question Books for Comprehension, SPaG and more

Available from all good booksellers, including:

cgpbooks.co.uk   amazon.co.uk   WHSmith   Waterstones